A DANCE
IN THE DARK

Discovering Hidden Treasures In Life's Darkest Valleys

Stacy Fulton

WESTBOW
P R E S S
A DIVISION OF THOMAS NELSON

Unless otherwise indicated, all scripture quotations are taken from the Holy Bible, New Living Translation, copyright © 1996. Used by permission of Tyndale House Publishers, Inc., Wheaton, Illinois 60189. All rights reserved.

Scripture quotations taken from the Amplified® Bible, Copyright © 1954, 1958, 1962, 1964, 1965, 1987 by The Lockman Foundation Used by permission.

Scripture quotations marked (CEV) are from the Contemporary English Version Copyright © 1991, 1992, 1995 by American Bible Society, Used by Permission.

Scripture taken from The Message. Copyright © 1993, 1994, 1995, 1996, 2000, 2001, 2002. Used by permission of NavPress Publishing Group.

WestBow Press books may be ordered through booksellers or by contacting:

WestBow Press
A Division of Thomas Nelson
1663 Liberty Drive
Bloomington, IN 47403
www.westbowpress.com
1-(866) 928-1240

ISBN: 978-1-4497-5173-9 (sc)
ISBN: 978-1-4497-5174-6 (hc)
ISBN: 978-1-4497-5172-2 (e)

Library of Congress Control Number: 2012908333

Printed in the United States of America

WestBow Press rev. date: 05/17/2012

For Jesus
My life, my heart, my everything… it's all for You

For my four loves - Ron, Jeremiah, Charlie and Taylor
You are my treasures

For every woman battling the pain of infertility
Joy does come in the mourning

CONTENTS

ACKNOWLEDGEMENTS

To my husband, Ron…thank you for being my best friend, my strong arm and my biggest fan. None of this would be possible without your support and your love. It is an honor to be your wife. Thank you for leading our family and for encouraging me to put my "yes" on the table. Living and experiencing life with you is the best. Thank you for showing me what the love of Jesus looks like through your selfless and unconditional love for me. I see Jesus in you and it makes me love you all the more. You're the greatest, Pal.

To my children, Jeremiah, Charlie and Taylor…thank you for making me a mom. I'm so honored that God gave me each of you. You are my gifts straight from the Father. I can't imagine anything in this world better than waking up to your smiles everyday. Thank you for bringing my heart so much joy that it feels like it could explode. It is an honor to be called your mom.

To my Trinity Church family…thank you for walking me through one of the hardest times of my life. I can't imagine what my journey would have looked like without you all as a part of it. Jim and Becky, I am forever grateful for the support and encouragement you gave me. Shelia, there will never be enough words to say thank you for your leadership and your wisdom along the way. To all my friends too many to list, I love you. Trinity Church will forever be etched into the depths of my heart.

To my mom and dad and sister…thank you for loving me and encouraging me to pursue my dreams. I can't imagine life without you. What a blessing to be born into our family. I love you.

To Lori, Shana and Courtney…thank you for reading this manuscript before it ever came to be published and for believing that it actually could be. Your love and encouragement has been my rock along the way. The day He brought each of you into my life is a special gift all on it's own. Thank you for your support and your prayers. I am humbled that I get to call you my friends. I love you more than I could ever say.

To my band of sisters…(you know who you are)…Thank you for bathing my life and this book in prayer. I love serving Jesus with you. I love you.

To Sally…thank you for being used of God to edit this book. Your dedication to pray and seek the heart of God as you poured over this book is priceless to me. You are my angel.

To my Highland Park pastors…Brett, thank you for pouring the Word into my life and providing me opportunities to be used of God. Jeff, thank you for inspiring me to not settle for quiet perfection, but to go for epic in all that I do.

To my Highland Park family…thank you for being a safe place. Thank you for loving my family and giving us a home. It is an honor to worship Jesus with each of you. I love you all.

To my Abba Father…my thanks to You is given by my life. I stand in awe of a love so great that You would include me in something so much bigger than myself. Words do not express the thankfulness in my heart for Your grace and patience with me through the process of life. You are my everything. Saying yes to You has taken me on the greatest journey of my life. All of this is for You, Jesus. Every word.

FOREWARD

Principles and precepts leave faith sterile and stoic. That's why the bible colors our faith with stories of Joseph, Daniel, Esther and others. Who among us has never imagined the raw emotion of David facing Goliath, cowardly brothers peeking from their caves, or the exultant joy victory achieved? Who can read about Joseph's reunion with his rascal brothers without wiping a tear from our eye? Or, Who hasn't gained strength and perspective from spending a night with Daniel in his lion's den? But all the heroes of faith aren't ancient.

Stacy Fulton skillfully and with great spiritual depth, unveils her story of faith's process in a way that challenges and inspires. A Dance in the Dark candidly discovers and unveils emotion, fears, and eventually grace which not only sustains her, but transforms.

My wife and I enjoyed the privilege of participating in the story you are about to read. As Ron and Stacy's pastor, we watched this young couple cultivate a Christian testimony, engage as effective church leaders, while agonizing over unmet expectations and unanswered questions. We attended the funeral for their dreams and joyously celebrated when those dreams resurrected from the dead.

Adversity and death of our dreams make demands on our relationship with God which, at the time, seems irreparable. When God orders our life without taking time to explain Himself, believers become angry and distant, even if publically we're still able to put on a pretty face. Stacy's story provides fabric for our fears and misunderstandings by showing how they become a canvas on which God artistically engineers life.

Christian faith is an extrapolation of insights regarding how Jesus loves us, died for us, rose again and promises to return. Explanations and doctrines certainly seem required as we try to anchor our faith in storms. But when you meet a friend who learned her dance in life's darkest places, true impartation is often the result. <u>A Dance in the Dark</u> imparts hope.

Jim Hennesy,
Senior Pastor of Trinity Church, Cedar Hill, TX
Author of "No More Cotton Candy"

THE JOURNEY

Introduction

Are you ready to dance?

I'm not talking the kind of dancing that requires you to get up and do a "two-step" or "electric slide." No, I'm talking about a dance that is something totally different. It's a dance that takes place in moments you would least expect to be dancing. I'm talking about a dance that will radically transform the way you view shattered dreams, broken hearts, times of uncertainty, or divine interruptions. I'm talking about a holy dance that takes place with you and an audience of One.

One of my very favorite verses in the Bible is Jeremiah 29:13 that says, "You will find Me, when you seek Me with all of your heart." I love it because it evokes something more than just a promise. It evokes the start of a journey, a journey with the promise of finding what we are searching for.

When I got saved, I set out on a journey. I wanted to know God. I wanted to serve Him. I wanted to be all that He created me to be. I was a sophomore in college the day I found myself at an altar at a small Baptist church in Florence, Alabama. All I knew that day was that my life was nothing. I was empty and hopeless and He met me that Sunday morning and gave me new life.

At first, I thought I just wanted normal. I thought I just wanted to attend church and be happy with the fact that I was saved and going to heaven. But that all changed as I began to grow spiritually. I became dissatisfied with just being a Christian. Deep inside, my heart was longing for more than I was seeing. I didn't really understand that at the time, but looking back now, I can see that He was drawing me deeper before I even realized what He was doing. And He was drawing me through worship.

I've always loved worship since the day I got saved. However, my definition of the term has drastically changed since then.

I used to define worship as "music." You know, the fast songs we sang during our church service were "praise," and the slow songs we sang were the "worship." And THAT became what I thought worship was—singing a slow song in church. I thought that the only time I "worshipped" was when I came to church on Sunday and we sang our slow songs. I thought finding God consisted of how the music portion of the service went that particular Sunday. I thought I had missed out if we didn't sing any songs that touched my heart or that I really liked, because I didn't get to really "worship" that day. Boy did I have it all wrong.

No wonder my life has been full of ups and downs spiritually.

I used to wonder why I could be so on fire one day and then shortly after the fire would have fizzled out. I always found myself on this spiritual roller coaster of emotions, that usually ended with a longer period of me being "off" than me being "on" spiritually. Ever been there?

It wasn't until my life came face to face with the fact that I had some misguided notions about what it meant to worship Christ that everything changed.

You see, what I didn't realize is that my worship was based on how good things were going in my life. So, when things were good, I could go in to church on Sunday and let loose in those slow songs and leave feeling like I had "entered in" because I sang those songs with all my heart. I mean, that's what Jesus wanted from me...right? To sing when life was good? To raise my hands when I was walking in abundance and blessing?

The problem came when I started feeling dry. The problem came when life wasn't so happy. You know, those times when we find that our gushy feelings have gone AWOL and we are left on a Sunday morning with no feeling, no emotion, and a set of songs that mean nothing because everything is based on our feelings! It's these times when the hands stay down to my side, my heart is heavy, and I feel no reason to even sing.

I'd like to say that it only took me a few months after being saved to learn that this way of thinking was obviously wrong. However, it has taken me several years, and several times of coming face to face with the reality of WHO God is before I have truly come to understand what worship is.

The truth? I learned what worship was in the darkest moments of my life. Sure, I could sing loudly and raise my hands when everything was going great. I could acknowledge how wonderful God was and could believe that He was worthy of all my praise. That was easy. But what happened when things didn't turn out like I had hoped? What happened when there were no "feel good" moments because life had gotten hard? What happened when my beliefs were challenged? Had

God changed because of my circumstances? Was He any less "good" just because my life wasn't? The reality was, no, but my ability to worship said otherwise. My worship then began to be challenged. When I didn't have a reason to worship, I didn't worship. When I didn't have a reason to sing, I didn't sing. And my spiritual roller coaster showed it all too well.

My worship was dictated by my circumstances, when the truth is, my worship should've been dictated by WHO my God was. Sadly, it took some painful moments in some dark places for me to realize that truth.

As you will read in this book, my dark circumstances came about through infertility. Whatever the circumstance, though, we all come face to face with this reality at some point in our journey with Christ. We each have to discover the truths to be found in our darkest nights. While I found mine in the inability to have a child, anyone who battles a broken heart or shattered dream will have the same opportunity.

Through my journey, I learned that worship doesn't happen on Sunday morning when I sing a certain slow song. Worship happens, instead, everyday of my life, as I choose to honor God in the midst of my pain. Worship happens when I choose to turn my eyes toward heaven and declare that He is good and worthy of my praise, even when everything around me has crumbled. Worship happens as I step out onto the dance floor of adversity and dance face to face with the one Who takes my ashes and turns them into something beautiful again.

Once I learned the true meaning of worship, my life has been ruined for anything less. I no longer run from painful moments and desert times. Instead, I know that He has something awaiting me on the other side of these places that will far outweigh the tears that it takes to get there. I now more fully understand how we find Him when we search for Him with all of our heart. It takes all of our heart to worship Him in the midst of difficulties. However we DO find Him. I learned that first hand. And so can you.

Hidden beneath these lowest places, these darkest valleys, are His treasures awaiting to be found. Hidden beneath the rubble and ashes in our lives we find the greatest treasure of all—His heart. The question is, how do we uncover these treasures? How do we find Him in the midst of it all? How do we uncover His heart in the worst of times?

We uncover them through our worship. We uncover them when we dance.

So, I ask you again—are YOU ready to dance?

Chapter 1

HIDDEN TREASURES

"I will give you treasures hidden in the darkness,
riches hidden in the secret places." Isaiah 45:3

I FIRST STARTED WRITING this book almost ten years ago. I started writing because I was thrust head first into a place that was new territory for me spiritually. I found myself at the bottom of a pit. So I wrote. I wanted to remember the experience, the path I never thought I'd be walking. I loved to journal, so I just began to pour my heart into putting down on paper what was actually happening to my heart, to my dreams.

Everyone has dreams. Some are big and some are small. Some are possible and some are just unrealistic. Some people dream of being a famous superstar, such as an actor/actress, sports figure, etc... Others dream of that corner office on the top floor with the great view and fat paycheck. They dream of owning their own business and making it rich. Or perhaps your dream is to travel to a different country and see new things.

And still, others dream of meeting that special someone who will make all their dreams come true. My dream? Well, my dream was simple. I just wanted to have a baby.

Now to most women, this is a natural dream. As women, we want the joy of creating something together with our spouses that is part of us both. We long to hear children call us mother, to hold them in our arms, and to look at them and see our eyes or our husband's smile. It's just natural. And this was my dream. I wanted to be a mom.

My husband and I were married in January 1996. As a matter of fact, we've just celebrated our sixteenth anniversary as I'm writing this book. Our marriage hasn't always been perfect, but it's been steady and above all, it has been good. At the time we were married we were both attending school at Christ For the Nations in Dallas, Texas. We graduated in May of 1997 and moved back to our hometown in Alabama to work at a church. In September of that year, we made the choice most married couples makes at some point eventually. We decided it was time to start our family.

I can still remember that night as we lay there talking about it. My heart was flooded with every emotion under the sun. I was going to be a mom. ME! I was going to have a little girl or little boy and I was going to be a mother. I could hardly contain my joy!

We decided not to tell anyone at the time because we wanted the news of our pregnancy to be a big surprise. I was already planning how I would tell my parents our big announcement. But soon, days turned into weeks, and weeks turned into months. And there was nothing. We had moved back to Texas in 1998, so we no longer had family around. I had actually begun telling a few close friends at this point, so I would have someone to be excited with me about the journey and possibilities that lay ahead of me in parenthood. I would swear them to secrecy so as not to let out our big secret.

As the weeks and months passed, we came up short every month. My life soon became a roller coaster of emotions. I would always tell myself THIS would be our lucky month. And then it would come and go with still no positive pregnancy test. There's no telling how many tests I bought because with the slightest suspicion of being pregnant I would whip out a home pregnancy test to see if my suspicions were true. With every negative result, my heart began to sink within me.

It had been a couple years since we started trying, and most of our friends knew by this time. Anyone who was close to me knew I was on pins and needles every month, just waiting. We had good friends and they always meant well, but I began to grow weary of the "encouragement" I would get. You know... "Just be patient, it'll happen when you're not stressing out over it"...."Why don't you just adopt?"...."Just relax".... NOT exactly the words a woman consumed with having a baby wants to hear when she is unsuccessful month after month.

I'll share my full story later on, but for now, I'll let you in on what was happening. I had begun a far greater journey and didn't realize it. You see, my life had taken a turn I wasn't expecting. I had been casually walking along through life, following Jesus, loving Jesus, pursuing Jesus, but never really "trusting" Jesus. I mean, sure, I had to trust Him to become my Savior—that's not the kind of trust I'm talking about. I'm talking about the kind of trust involved when life as you know it goes wrong. When your plans and your dreams are shattered. When you find yourself in complete darkness—I mean pitch black, can't-see-your-hand-in-front-of-your-face kind of darkness. When you find yourself viewing the world through a broken and wounded heart, trying to make sense of anything. Trying to make sense of God.

It's these times in our lives we'd rather avoid. When we think about the words of Isaiah 45:3, we aren't really excited about finding a treasure; we just want an escape. We are always so eager to find a light switch when we encounter darkness, but what if we knew there is something greater waiting to be found? What if, when we enter into these times, we chose to look at the darkness another way? What if we allowed God to be our guide through it, and ultimately lead us to a treasure we never would have known had we not "stumbled" upon this dark place?

Now, let me just say, I don't believe we "stumble" into darkness. We arrive there either by our own choices, by attacks of the enemy, or God's divine leading. Either way, if we approach it the right way, we will always come through darkness changed. I fully believe it.

> "Who among you fears the LORD and obeys his
> servant? If you are walking in darkness, without a ray
> of light, trust in the LORD and rely on your God."
> Isaiah 50:10

There's a key to navigating through darkness and the key is Jesus. The key is found in trusting Jesus. You can't see when you are in the dark, so you have to allow Him to lead you or else you could be in trouble. After all, He's the only One who knows where the paths lead and He's the only One who knows where the pitfalls are along the way. It's when we choose not to grab hold of His hand during these trials that we find ourselves in trouble. Without His guidance, we are prone to run into obstacles, fall into pits and get completely turned around, unable to find our way. If we're holding on to Him, then we save ourselves the trouble of running into them. He will be our guide. He gives us His promise in Isaiah 48:17:

> "I am the LORD your God, who teaches
> you what is good for you and leads you
> along the paths you should follow."

He WILL lead. We just have to choose to follow Him when our lives take unexpected turns.

Every significant character in the Bible faced this same scenario. They encountered trials. They encountered suffering. They encountered uncharted territory. They encountered some form of darkness or another. They were all faced with the same choice that we are: either to trust God and follow His leading, or attempt to sail the unknown on their own. Their situations all presented some great challenges, but that's what makes their stories so great. They all found themselves in a position to join an epic story being written by the very hand of God. They were just ordinary people who trusted God and became extraordinary examples.

When you find yourself in places you weren't expecting, when you find yourself in the middle of a fierce storm, when you find yourself in the blackest darkness, just remember you are not alone. Consider Paul. Consider David. Consider Abraham. And Hanna. And Moses. And Joseph. And Jonah. Consider all the great heroes of the faith when you come face to face with uncertain times. Their stories are meant to help guide us. That's why Hebrews gives us an entire chapter about faith. All of

Hebrews 11 is about men and women who walked in complete faith and allowed God to lead as they followed. They show us what following God through uncharted territory looks like. They show us what following God when they don't understand His ways looks like. They show us example after example of what it means to trust when you can't see. This chapter in Hebrews points to our ultimate example, which is Christ Himself.

The Message words it perfectly:

> Do you see what this means—all these pioneers who blazed the way, all these veterans cheering us on? It means we'd better get on with it. Strip down, start running—and never quit! No extra spiritual fat, no parasitic sins. Keep your eyes on Jesus, who both began and finished this race we're in. Study how he did it. Because he never lost sight of where he was headed—that exhilarating finish in and with God—he could put up with anything along the way: Cross, shame, whatever. And now he's there, in the place of honor, right alongside God. When you find yourselves flagging in your faith, go over that story again, item by item, that long litany of hostility he plowed through. That will shoot adrenaline into your souls!
> Hebrews 12:1-3

So there it is, our treasure map, perfectly laid out with all the examples and testimonies we need, full of truth and wisdom in every way. Our ultimate treasure map is God's Word, and I was about to need it like never before.

I didn't know I was about to live Isaiah 45:3 just like all those people in Hebrews.

The date was June 7, 2001. It had been over three and a half years since we started trying to have a baby and my doctor had advised us to have some testing to see why nothing was happening. So on this day, as I was in my office at work, my phone rings. It's my husband and he has just spoken with the doctor who informed us that our hopes for a child were unrealistic. We had some weird issues going on and because of it, our chances of ever having a baby were unlikely. Even with medical intervention, our chances were slim to none. Thus my "journey" began through a dream that was shattered right before my eyes. We would never have children of our own.

Ever been there? Life as you knew it came to a screeching halt. Maybe you got the call you had been dreading from the doctor. Maybe you came home to an empty house after many years of what you thought was a happy marriage. Maybe that job you've worked at for all those years suddenly got cut. Maybe you said goodbye to a loved one, lay a child or spouse to rest. Maybe you got a letter of foreclosure because you haven't been able to make payments. Life just came to a screeching halt, and let's just be honest—it stinks.

You were happy. You were traveling along just fine, and then...BAM! Life got interrupted. You got detoured to a different path, but therein lies the adventure—that's when the real journey begins. Now, it may not seem like an adventure at the time. If you're like me, you kick and scream for quite a while at first because you didn't ask for this. But when the kicking and screaming subsides and the panic gives way to the journey, the darkness reveals an opportunity to seize the Father's heart and walk away forever changed.

You've always heard, "Life isn't fair." And that's true - life isn't fair. But when we belong to Christ, when we are walking with Him, it doesn't matter if life is fair. Why? Because the God we cling to is JUST. He is the Author of a story we have yet to imagine. He writes pages full of adventure, and heroism and triumphs. He writes stories with endings that are beyond epic, filled with redemption and truly glorious. Yet in His great love for His children, He also writes pages in our stories that are filled with uncertainty, with questions, and yes, dark valleys. He does so because these pages in our stories cause us to seek after and pursue Him. And when we pursue Him, we find Him; and in the process, we become more like Him. Sure, we could get stuck on asking Him "Why?" But then we just begin to miss out on the real adventure, and on the greater story at hand.

An important thing we have to remember is that disappointments don't just have to be huge and earth shattering to rock our world. They can be smaller things that happen that God uses to detour us off the path we are on. It's just things that take us by surprise, change our plans and force us to reset the navigation tool in our life.

One thing always remains for sure though, and that is that disappointments and shattered dreams cause a shift in our reality. They alter our plans and sometimes, they end up defining our lives. Ask anyone who has gone through some major trial and they will probably tell you that they are not the same person they were before the troubles came. Sometimes that's good, and sometimes that's bad. It all depends on the roads they choose AFTER the detour happens that gives us the definition.

We never choose to have a detour in our life. I never chose to walk the path I found myself walking towards. But looking back, I see the hand of God in every little detail. In every tear. In every painful moment. He was there. He was shaping me, cleansing me, and completely redefining me.

Chapter 2

PREPARE FOR BATTLE

"Praise the LORD, who is my rock. He trains my
hands for war and gives my fingers skill for battle."
Psalm 144:1

DID YOU KNOW THAT you're in the midst of a great battle?
Every day, in each chapter of your life-story, the battle rages.
We have an enemy who is bent on our destruction. He seeks
only to steal, kill and destroy—to murder—the saints of God.
So, dear friend, suit up, because this enemy is after you; and
when your path detours off the main road, and you are going
down what appears to be a lonely, fearful path, that's when he
will launch his greatest attack against you as a child of God. His
attack begins subtly; it approaches quietly. He patiently sows
seeds of doubt because one of his greatest weapons is against
your trust, against your faith, against all that you know and
hold dear about your Father God. The enemy watches and waits
for that perfect moment until you are vulnerable and weak,
and then he pounces violently. He seeks to knock you down

and once you're down, he unleashes with ancient ferocity to keep you there. It is carefully planned. It comes when you least expect it. He is crafty, but he does not have to be victorious.

When we got the news that we would never be able to have children, I was knocked down emotionally, spiritually, physically—you name it. Everything I had been dreaming of had just been destroyed, and it was time to find closure. Receiving the news provided a means to begin the grieving process of a death in my life. And that's exactly what it was—a death. It was the death of a dream. It was the death of something that was such a part of me, it was like having to bury a friend. So that's what I did. I had to grieve, but instead of providing closure, my grief soon got the best of me in more ways than one.

There were days I would have a hard time getting out of bed because I had become so depressed. I felt as if someone had picked me up and dropped me into a deep, dark hole with no way of escape. I felt hopeless and lost and all alone. Nothing I did to try to help myself worked, and it was here, in this moment the enemy chose to launch his attack against me. He did it by sowing doubts of my Heavenly Father's love for me.

I had been saved for ten years when this happened. I thought I was a fairly strong Christian. I loved God. I was faithful in my service to Him. I thought a whole lot of other "lofty" things about my faith up until this point; but when the attack began, Satan began to destroy my faith with hisses of doubt.

I heard whispers in the night that said, "If God really loved you He would've given you a baby"; "The Bible tells you to be fruitful and multiply yet you are incapable. God must have not meant *you* in that scripture"; "You can't really trust God with your dreams because He will let you down." I heard these lies over and over and over again until finally, I started believing them. I actually began to question God. I questioned His love for me. I thought He was just looking down on me playing a sick joke as He taunted me with the desire for a child and slapped me in the face with the inability to conceive one. And I became angry. So angry, in fact, that I stormed off on a lonely desert road that led to the edge of deep, dark, and bottomless pit.

I remember those dark days. I felt so hopeless around all of my friends. People didn't really know how to approach me because I was just a basket case. I hated special occasions that had anything to do with babies or parents, especially baby showers. I caused quite a scene at one baby shower in particular. I'll never forget it and I'm sure my friend won't, either. I had such good intentions. I was determined to go and support my friend and celebrate her baby. I was actually doing fine at first. I'm not sure at what moment that changed, but all I know is, I made a quick dash to the bathroom where I called another friend and told her of my dilemma. She advised me to suddenly come down with a migraine and get out of there as fast as I could. I finally unlocked the bathroom and came out to find my friend and her mom. Instead of using the migraine excuse though, I just told them the truth. The mother hugged me, told me she understood and quickly escorted me to the back door without drawing attention so I could leave unnoticed. They said they would use the cover of the migraine to tell anyone who had asked about me after that. I've never forgotten that day and what it meant for them to be so understanding.

Church was pure torture for me. Mother's Day services, baby dedications, Father's Day—they all just screamed out that I would never be able to take part in these celebrations and that made me want to withdraw from church altogether. My saving grace at this point was that I was actually working at the church we attended and so I kind of "had" to go to church. I guess God knew what He as doing in setting that up, huh? I love His sense of humor and how He works so cleverly without us having a clue to what He's doing!

Do you see how the enemy was working? He was using all of these circumstances and incidents to just try and build his case against me. During every baby dedication at church, he would sit and whisper those same lies in my ears, and I listened until they finally began to take hold in my heart. I started to believe every word of his lies. Thinking back on that now, I can only imagine how God must have felt to see me fall prey to the enemy's schemes. And even more so, it hurts me to think how His heart must have broken when He saw me exchange truth for lies about His goodness.

All of this eventually led me down that dreadful desert path. I allowed the enemy to blind me to the point of following him toward destruction.

There are often times in our lives when we go through something that causes us to follow blindly. The enemy will use anything he can to take our focus off of Jesus and instead, convince us to focus on lies. The lies lead us astray time after time and convince us to run as hard as we can away from God.

I was running hard down a dangerous path that was leading me to a decision that, if I chose wrongly, would have meant certain spiritual death. I was faced with a choice - to continue on with Jesus and trust Him through this darkness; or turn my back on Him and choose another direction that didn't include Him at all. It would mean forsaking all I knew about Him to commit spiritual suicide.

I know it sounds terrible to have had all these thoughts, but I was tired. I was really tired. So the thought of quitting altogether sounded much better than persevering. Ever been there?

The whole thing reminds me of marathon training.

I started running a few years ago to lose weight and get healthy. Before I knew it, I had discovered "the runner's high" and was completely obsessed with it. I started out doing short races, like your occasional 5k's, but soon found myself desiring the more prestigious half marathons and ultimately, a full marathon.

I began running in March, and by the end of the summer, I had registered for my first half marathon. Once I completed that, I was hooked. I was consumed with running and completing a marathon. After all, that's a runner's ultimate prize—to complete a marathon and showcase that "26.2" sticker on the back of your vehicle. That sticker carries a lot of pride!

I began training for the marathon in September. I had registered for a race that was the second weekend in December, and was working with a running coach who set up a training plan for me to follow.

Each week I had a certain number of miles to get in and with each week, the mileage increased. There was always a long run included, which also increased each week. The eventual goal was to complete a twenty one mile long run at some point within the training.

Long runs are hard. You start out with short distances, such as twelve or thirteen miles. Then each week it increases. The interesting thing about long runs, though, is that each week there comes a point during the run where you think you can't go another step. Your body reaches its capacity. Without fail, every time, your body will want to shut down. But each week as you complete those long runs, once you hit the point where you ended the week before, it isn't nearly as hard as the first time you did it. But after you hit that point, it is hard to keep pushing to the end of this run.

For example, lets say last week your long run was fourteen miles. It was tough as nails to get to that point if you'd never ran that many miles before. But, you made it. You finished it. And this week, your long run is fifteen miles. It's amazing how when you reach the fourteen mile marker this week, you feel great. It's just that last mile that gets you every time. It's always tougher because it's new territory. It requires you to push yourself farther than you've been before, and it's hard. You are at your weakest because you are tired.

In all of my training runs, the longest I ever ran was twenty miles. That's a whole six miles short of a marathon, but, they say adrenaline will carry you through those last several miles on race day. I sure hoped so because those twenty miles were a boogar!

I did all my training and marathon day finally arrived. I stepped up to the starting line full of adrenaline. I started out at a good steady pace and was running well. It was about mile twenty-one when the real fatigue started setting in.

I can still remember calculating all the miles I still had left. I tried to break it down like a shorter practice run. But none of my attempts seemed to negate the fact that my legs felt like they were about to fall off and my body wanted to collapse on the side of the road.

The other thing that really stood out to me was all the other runners. When the race first started, everyone was talking and enjoying everyone's company along the way. We made friends with strangers. It was great. And there were large groups of people still together. Up until these last few miles that is. All of a sudden, people were becoming scarce. No one was talking after about mile twenty four. It was as if I had entered a war zone. Every person fighting with all they had to make it to the finish line. Everyone was exhausted. It was hard.

While those few miles were tough, it was that last mile that was the toughest. Our minds played tricks on us. Our legs wanted to collapse. Our whole body wanted to kill over and die. We just wanted to quit. We each had to force ourselves to continue. After all, there was just that "1.2 miles" left! We had come this far, we had to finish!

Needless to say, I did make it. I crossed the finish line and got that medal I had been dreaming about. I put the bumper sticker on my car. I was part of the club now. Some call it the stupidity club, others call it "THE" club. Regardless, I was there. I was in.

Now, I tell you all of that to really say one thing. Just like those long runs were hard and tiring and at the most crucial point in the marathon I was exhausted and wanted to give up, I now found myself running a spiritual marathon, and again I was tempted to quit. It looks easier to quit than keep going. It is easier to just throw in the towel. It's easier to sit down and give up than it is to fight and push through to the end. And this is where I was in my life. Do I fight or give up? Do I keep running or quit the race? It was my choice that I had to make.

It's a choice you'll have to make in your journey.

Before we explore what continuing on the path with Jesus looks like, lets stop for a bit and see what really happens if we make the choice to jump at this point and take that different path with the enemy. Let's see what it looks like to give up and quit. We'll call this "the pit".

The pit is just what it says—a pit. For the time being, it looks easy, less painful. It looks like it requires much less energy or devotion from us. But what is it really? The pit is a journey without God. It's the road you take when you say, "Enough God. I will do this myself. I will take control over my life, my destiny and won't include You in any part of it again. I will do it my way." At first, this road looks relatively painless. Let's face it, you've already been given a dose of pain than you ever cared to receive when your dream got shattered in the first place. So, anything that can alleviate that pain now looks pretty good. But, sad to say, that's just the appearance this pit gives.

When I was standing at this crossroad trying to make my decision, I had some big decisions to make. I was so angry at God. I had to decide if I was going to let my anger be enough to make me decide to run my life without Him or if I would allow Him to come into my anger and walk through the process with me. The thought of doing it without Him was looking good from the viewpoint of my flesh. I was tempted to push the pedal to the floor and drive straight into the heart of darkness alone, into the pit. The pit seemed bottomless, easier, less painful.

I had chased mirages and fallen into pits before. Before I got saved, my past included a lot of junk. Like most of us, I was good at being a sinner. It was so easy to drown my life in sinful habits. Those habits were the first place I turned when things were bad.

My heart was hurting from dealing with these infertility issues. I was in pain. It consumed me. I wasn't able to concentrate, I couldn't sleep, I was consumed with it all. I felt so betrayed by

God. My anger was building by the day. So this low road for me would have meant turning back to old habits in my life. Habits that could've destroyed me except for the grace of God. I knew the dangers of what this meant, yet looking over the edge at it now, it just looked like the easiest place to go and deal with what I was experiencing. I knew if I went back to old habits I could at least "feel good" for a bit. I didn't care how long. I just wanted some relief for my pain.

I also thought it looked good because I knew God wouldn't approve and it would go against what He wanted me to be doing. I was looking into the face of deep rebellion. It was a pit of darkness ruled by the prince of darkness himself. Here I was, this sweet little Christian girl who supposedly loved God, actually entertaining the thought of jumping right into a deep, dark pit. It was a deliberate freefall from grace.

Your pain will be very intense at times when you go through things. There will be times when it will consume you. So intense actually, that you'll be tempted to seek relief in places you never imagined. It's easy for that pain to turn into a rebellious fury. Let me clarify something about anger first, though. I'm not saying you can't be angry when you go through hard times; anger is part of a natural grieving process. But, when that anger begins to consume you, it becomes more than a grieving process—it becomes sin. In your grief you will experience anger. It's natural. It's natural to cry out to God for understanding and to feel betrayed. He wants us to bring those emotions to Him. However, once we let that anger control us and we can't get past it, then it moves from grief to controlling us, then it has become sin in our lives. If you are still thrusting your fist at God and everyone else in your life, you might have stepped into sin. Any anger that isn't dealt with through Jesus can make your journey a living hell. And that's basically what this dark pit is. It's a living hell. If we purposefully choose to abandon God because of our anger towards Him, we are handing over the keys to our freedom to the enemy.

So this is the "pit", this is the low road. It is paved, covered and led by darkness and death. While it looks good for a bit, it is filled with nothing but pure death. Our enemy, being one set on trying to kill, steal and destroy us, knows if he can get us believing his lies about this place and get us to make the leap, he will have taken us out of the battle altogether. He wins.

The enemy loves to put us on the run. Especially when he has us running from God. Like I mentioned before, I know what it's like to run. But when you run you are always looking forward, running towards something. On the contrary, when we are running "from" God, we aren't looking forward. We are constantly looking backward to make sure He hasn't caught us yet. The pit is just running from God. It's choosing to rebel against His authority and all He is. The pit only happens because we choose to believe lies over truth.

Simba learned this the hard way.

One of my favorite movies is "The Lion King". I love lions anyway, but put them in a movie and I'm completely in awe. In this particular movie, it's all about Simba and him coming into the throne that he was destined to receive when his father, Mufasa, passed on. However it didn't go quite that easy. All because Simba had an enemy named Scar who wanted the throne for himself. So he set Simba up and fed him lies to keep him from realizing truth, thus causing Simba to run away from what was rightfully his. Instead of walking into kingship,

Simba ran away from all he knew, into slavery. It wasn't slavery to *someone*; it was slavery to his past, to the lies he believed. They altered his life and nearly cost him his destiny. All because he believed lies over the truth.

This is why it is so important that we stay suited up spiritually. You never know when your life is going to be altered by some disappointment or roadblock you weren't expecting. So when these things occur, if you are grounded in the truth of God's word, it won't be such an easy task for the enemy to convince you that his lies are truth. You will know the truth before the lie ever makes it to your heart.

That's one reason why I love the story of Joseph. Like you and I, Joseph had a dream as well. In Genesis 37, we see that God gave Joseph a dream. A few dreams, actually. So Joseph did what most of us do: he went and told people. He told his brothers and his family to be exact. Problem was, his brothers were not excited about the dream like Joseph was. That's because Joseph's dream was a prophecy about him becoming ruler and his brothers being subject to him. Granted, this was probably a dream Joseph should have kept to himself, don't you think? But, he didn't, and the people who hated him most, hated his dream even more.

Sound like someone else we know? Sounds like the enemy to me. He hates us. He hates our God-given dreams even more. So what did Josephs brothers do? They devised a plan to destroy him. And what was the first thing they did? They threw him into a PIT.

Deciding that they didn't want to actually be the ones to kill him, they noticed some Ishmaelite traders coming their way. So, they decided to sell him to them as they passed by. When they took Joseph into Egypt, the Ishmaelite traders ended up selling him to Potiphar, who was an officer of Pharaoh, the king of Egypt. Genesis 39:2 reveals, "The Lord was with Joseph and blessed him greatly as he served in the home of the Egyptian master."

I think it's safe to say that unless Joseph was a faithful servant first to the Lord, he would not be blessed by the Lord. The Lord certainly wouldn't be with him in all he did. Yet, He was. And He did. He blessed him with abundant favor, even though Joseph's circumstances became hard. He was wrongly accused and thrown into prison. However, the bible tells us that the Lord was with Joseph even in prison.

I believe the Lord was with him because Joseph was faithful to Him. He was true to the God he believed and worshipped. When things started going wrong, he could've done it all differently. When his brothers threw him into the pit and then sold him into slavery he could've become angry and bitter and turned his back on the God who was giving him dreams. But he didn't. And God blessed him for it. Joseph didn't choose the pit, it was just the plan the enemy had for him to thwart the dream that God had given him. But here's what I want you to see: Joseph chose to do things a little differently. He chose to stay on the caravan that led him into Egypt.

This "caravan" is part of our journey as well. You see, one thing I have learned in my christian walk is that we all have dreams. Sometimes they happen like we hope they would. Sometimes the path to get there is a whole lot different than what we expected. Yet by choosing to stay on this caravan, we end up making it to our dreams fulfilled. But it is this "choosing", this "choice", that we are all faced with in our struggles that determines where the caravans take us specifically.

On a caravan being shipped off to Egypt—that's where I was. The enemy, despising my God-given dream of being a mother, shackled me with distrust and sold me as a slave. I was exhausted and tired. I was ready to quit. Quitting seemed a lot easier than continuing to follow Christ. The enemy was using old habits and all of his lies to draw me away from the loving embrace of my Father. He had been steady and constant in his attack on my soul. He waited patiently, hiding out of sight until he had me in his view. He was ready to make the shot to take me out. But, just like Joseph, I had a choice to make: to be carried off unwillingly, doubled over in disgust and hatred of God; or, to choose to stay on the caravan and know that my Father was holding the reins.

This wasn't the end but just the beginning of what He had planned. While I couldn't understand what He was doing, He was ready to do a work in me beyond my wildest dreams. He was ready to take me places I had never been. I was still in the darkness, but I had been there long enough that my eyes were beginning to adjust; and ever so gradually I began to see Him, my Father, who dispels the darkness. He was standing as a lighthouse amidst a terrifying storm, shining His light to guide my way. He was inviting me to journey with Him.

Chapter 3

STAY ON THE CARAVAN

"God made my life complete when I placed all the
pieces before Him. When I got my act together, He gave
me a fresh start. Now I'm alert to God's ways; I don't
take God for granted. Every day I review the ways He
works; I try not to miss a trick. I feel put back together,
and I'm watching my step. God rewrote the text of my
life when I opened the book of my heart to His eyes."
Psalm 18:20-24 The Message

DURING THE MONTHS FOLLOWING, I continued to
battle the pains of battered emotions. I had bought every book
I could find on dealing with infertility. I bought books on
adoption. I joined online support groups. I tried everything I
could to make myself deal with the pain and bring resolution to
my heart. It helped sometimes just to know that there were lots
of other people out there like me. Women who were dealing
with the same pain, the same frustrations, day in and day out. It

didn't relieve what I was going through, but it did bring some comfort to know that they were hurting just like I was.

It wasn't until I attended a conference in Dallas during January of 2002 that something happened. The conference was being put on by one of the authors of a book I had read on infertility and really connected with through it. I saw this and immediately knew I should go. It was just a one day thing, so I decided I could give up a Saturday to go hear someone talk about infertility in the hopes that maybe I'd find closure there. I had some friends who were walking through this same thing, so we all decided to go together.

I can still remember walking into the room and seeing all the couples there. Couples who looked just like everyone else, yet they were couples dealing with the same thing I was. They were all battling infertility. Ronnie wasn't able to attend with me because of work commitments, so I was there alone with our friends. As soon as the speaker stood up and started talking, I felt a wave of emotions begin to come over me. This lady was speaking out loud every single thing that was going on inside of me. Every hurt, every fear, every emotion. She was laying it out right before me. No book had ever done it quite like that. But here, in this moment, she was taking a scalpel and opening up my soul. On this day, it was more than I could stand.

At the first sight of a break I made my way to another room and called Ronnie. I was so overwhelmed with emotion I knew I couldn't do this alone. As soon as he could get off of work he made his way to downtown Dallas to catch the last half of the seminar with me.

At the end of the conference we went out with some of our dearest friends that evening. They had two young girls whom I had just taken in as my own almost, because we were so close to them. I was already rather quiet that night, still processing all I had heard just hours earlier. At some point I had ended up back in the girls' bedroom with them, helping their mom put them to bed. We adults intended to play cards once the kids were tucked away, however, things didn't go as planned. As I was helping her put them to bed, one of the girls crawled into my lap and just hugged me. I lost it. At that exact moment all the emotions of the day flooded me. I realized that I would never have a little girl to come sit in my lap and tell me good night. I'd just always be the "aunt" or the "mom's best friend," but never a mom. And my heart was broken.

The next morning I woke up and was about to get ready for church. Before I could, though, I had an honest talk with God. Probably the most honest I had been since this journey began. I told Him that I could not go on with life as it had been. He either had to show up and do something, or else I could not keep going. I needed Him. I needed Him desperately.

We made our way to church to discover we had a guest speaker that morning. That man spoke a message that changed my life.

His topic for the morning was the story of Joseph. Yep, Joseph. He began to tell the story of how Joseph had a dream, yet the way his dream came about was not anything like what Joseph had planned. However, regardless of the circumstance, Joseph decided to stay on the caravan and eventually, that caravan led him to Egypt, to the king's palace where his dream and destiny would finally be fulfilled.

As I sat there, I hung on every word he said. He was speaking straight to my heart, and as I listened to him, I felt the Lord begin to speak so softly to me. He began to tell me that He knew I had dreams. He had given me the dreams. I had always dreamed of women's ministry and doing something for Him. He knew I dreamed of being a mother. Yet the way He was going to bring the dreams about wasn't going to be the way I had planned. But, if I would agree to stay on the caravan I was on, even though infertility was my driver at the time, He promised that this caravan was going to lead me to my destiny and a dream fulfilled. So that morning I made a choice. I made THE choice, the choice that kept me on the right path. The choice that kept me on the caravan. Boy am I glad I did, because choosing to stay on the caravan started the most incredible journey of my life.

I left the altar that day and never looked back. I went to the altar a broken and shattered little girl. I walked away from that altar with a hope and newfound strength. You see, God met me that morning. He didn't wait for me to clean up my act and get myself together emotionally. He didn't wait for me to find resolution to my infertility. Instead, He came and met me in the middle of my messiest time. He came and grabbed me up, put me in His lap, let me hear His heart, and feel His heartbeat. He wiped my tears and just let me linger until I was ready to go and face the things ahead of me. He didn't reveal a big master plan to me or show me all that was to come. Instead, He showed me the power of His love and grace that would cover me through it all. He let me look into His eyes and see "I Am." And I knew that He was all I would need.

It did not matter that I had questioned Him so much up to this point. He knows our human frailty. He knows that disappointments that break our hearts will cause us to fall. Especially if we aren't fully grounded in Him and His Word. But that morning, I didn't meet a Father who was disappointed in how I had handled things so far. I didn't find a Redeemer who was angry that I had even thought of walking away from all He did to redeem me. I didn't sit in the lap of a Father who was just waiting to punish me with infertility just because He could. No, that morning I met I Am, and I looked into the eyes of a merciful, loving Father, who wanted nothing more than to comfort His daughter and heal her broken heart. I met Abba Father that morning. The Father Who loves like no other and through that love, transforms us completely.

It's impossible to look into His eyes like I did that day and walk away the same way you came. It's completely impossible. You can't find a buried treasure that will change your life and just walk away from it. No, if you had been looking for treasure and finally found it, you'd grab it and leave. That's just what I did that day. I found a treasure I had been searching for in His eyes and I can honestly say, I haven't been the same since. I caught the gaze of my Savior and I found healing, redemption and restoration.

You know how when you are in a crowded room and as you're panning the room, you catch it. You catch the gaze of someone who is looking at you. You catch a gaze of someone you know. Well, that's what happened that morning. I caught His gaze.

From that point forward, I began to look at things differently than I had before. Was every day a walk in the park after that? No! There were days my heart still hurt. There were days I still cried. But, I didn't look at the situation as I had before. Before, I had looked at everything as hopeless. Today I look at everything through the eyes of hope. I see it through my Father's perspective. I went from an earthly view to a God's eye view.

Think of it this way…a little child in line at an amusement park. They can't see what's ahead of them or behind them. All they can see is the person in front of them or beside them. They have no idea where they are going because they can't see any further than the person smashed right in front of their face. They know they are inching their way towards the start of the line, but have no idea what it looks like. They keep going around the turns, but never able to see anything other than what they're able to see because of the place they are at. It's just their perspective. But something happens when the father picks the child up and puts them on his shoulders. They are able to see things differently. The pressing crowd no longer looks so scary and frightening because they are up above it. They have the ability to see much farther ahead than they could down on their level. They have their fathers view, his perspective.

Same thing with airplanes. Once we take off and leave the ground, even the tallest of buildings become small. All because our perspective changes when we get higher than the building is. The tallest building in the world looks like an ant from 30,000 feet in the air. That's exactly what God does for us when we allow Him to take us up to new heights and begin to soar above the problems we are facing. Giants don't look so big after all from where He is sitting. They are pretty small in His eyes. And He wants us to see things as He does. But we have to see them THROUGH His eyes.

This is what happened to me. Previously all I could see was the situation through my eyes and my perspective. But when I let Father come into the midst of my situation with me, He picked me up, put me on His shoulders and allowed me to see things from a different perspective. I began to see things through His eyes now. What once looked so scary now looked a lot smaller to me. All because my perspective changed.

Joseph had perspective. He kept his dream hidden in his heart even when times got tough. He stayed faithful to God no matter what happened around him. His caravan led him on some rough trails, but the roughest of roads didn't deter his heart away from God. I'm sure he didn't enjoy being betrayed by his brothers.

I'm sure he didn't enjoy being sold into slavery.

I'm sure he didn't enjoy being wrongly accused and thrown into prison.

But he was faithful. He found favor, even in prison, because God was with him and caused him to succeed in all he did, even when he was in places he didn't really want to be. He continued to serve in the dungeons of life. He had focus and determination to follow and serve God no matter where life had him, no matter the adversity. He chose to stay where he was and be faithful to God in the midst of it. He stayed on the caravan.

From my Father's shoulders, I can see that Joseph's adversity was a lot more than just adversity. It was training ground for his next assignment. His prisons were his divine interruptions that equipped him for God's call on his life. Our adversities are the same thing.

It was hard for me to see at the time, but all of this was doing the same thing for me as it had for Joseph. It was just training for the next thing. We learn to trust God through trials and tribulations. They form and shape our faith. We see God move on our behalf through something and it makes it easier to trust Him the next time. He uses the things in our life to train and equip us. He was equipping me for the bigger journey He had planned for my life whether I knew it or not. The moment I left that altar and submitted to the process, my real training began.

All of Joseph's sufferings eventually led him to Pharaoh. His sufferings led him to Egypt. Egypt represents slavery. It represents bondage. And Joseph was here for thirteen years according to Genesis 41.

Everything in his life had led up to this point, this place. He remained faithful to God in the hard times and through the dungeons, through all the captivity and bondage, and it all led him to a place of freedom and favor and blessing, and ultimately, his destiny.

> "And Pharaoh said to his servants, 'Can we find this man's equal, a man in whom is the spirit of God?' And Pharaoh said to Joseph, 'Forasmuch as your God has shown you all of this, there is nobody as intelligent and discreet and understanding and wise as you are. You shall have charge over my house, and all my people shall be governed according to your word, with reverent submission, and obedience. Only in matters of the throne will I be greater than you are. Then Pharaoh said to Joseph, 'See, I have set you over all the land of Egypt' and Pharaoh took off his signet ring from his hand and put it on Joseph's hand and arrayed him official vestments of fine linen and put a gold chain about his neck; He made him to ride in the second chariot which he had, and officials cried before him, 'Bow the knee!' And he set him over all the land of Egypt."
> Genesis 41:38-43

According to God's story about Joseph, we see that God brought Joseph into a place of favor and authority in due time. He blessed him with great responsibilities. If we remain faithful to God in the midst of our sufferings, greater blessings than we can imagine are on the other side. It's not our job to bring about our destiny. It's our job to make ourselves available to Him in every situation we find ourselves in, so that He can transform us and use our adversity to bring about His plans and purposes for us.

Also, notice that Joseph was put in charge of Egypt. The place that once enslaved him, he now ruled. I believe that's because God uses the places we walk and the things we go through to touch others. He uses what He brings us out of to minister to others. Time and time again, He takes the broken places in our lives and makes something absolutely beautiful from them.

A little further in Joseph's story, we see that he had children. I love the story and names behind his children. They teach us even more how adversity shapes us and what God is capable of doing through it.

> "And Joseph called the firstborn Manasseh, meaning
> 'making to forget', for he said, 'My God has made me
> forget all my toil and hardship and all my father's house.'
> And the second born he called Ephraim, meaning 'to
> be fruitful', for he said, 'my God has caused me to be
> fruitful in the land of my suffering and affliction."
> Genesis 41:51-52

Now THIS gets me all fired up! God shows us through the life of Joseph that He will bless us and cause us to forget all the troubles we have endured during those dark times and that He will cause us to be fruitful in the land of our sufferings. If that doesn't make you want to grab a stick and go running after the devil I don't know what will!

So what do we do in times of darkness? What do we do in adversity? We stay on the caravan. Joseph had dreams in his life that God had given him. He didn't get there the way he thought he would. At any given point in the process when things got hard, he could have made the choice to give up and turn his heart against God. But, he didn't. He chose to remain faithful even in the darkest moments of his life. And God rewarded his faithfulness. In the end, he did see his dreams fulfilled. His destiny did get fulfilled. But it was the JOURNEY he went on to get there that made him to be the powerful man of God that he was.

Joseph kept the ways of the Lord and did not depart from his God. This is how we must be as well. We must stay true to God in all of our ways. Yes, we hurt and we grieve, and that's okay. But in our grieving, we must keep our hearts before God and stay true to Him above the pain. We must stay vigilant, and refuse to allow our hearts to depart from Him.

Shattered dreams, dark valleys, adversities…these are truly the equipping and training grounds for the saints of God. They are the tools He uses to ready us to do the work He has called each of us to do. He fulfills the dreams He has given us or spoken over us. We have to remain faithful during the process and allow Him to redefine us and change us into vessels that He can use to bring about those dreams. Even when it seems the darkest hour is at hand, His purposes are being achieved in our lives. We just have to see with Father's perspective and not our own. Our eyes can only see circumstances, but His eyes see through the circumstances and past the pain and see the end result being birthed.

The grand finale of Joseph's story is great and actually the nugget of truth that we can all use to keep going through our current trials.

You know the story up to this point...his brothers did, in fact, have to come to him for help and he did not reveal his identity to them as they all thought their brother was dead. But, in due time, he did reveal to his brothers who he was. What he said to them at this point is what makes me love this story all the more.

> "But now, don't be upset, and don't be angry with
> yourselves for selling me to this place. It was God
> who sent me here ahead of you to preserve your lives.
> This famine that has ravaged the land for two years
> will last five more years and there will be neither
> plowing nor harvesting. God has sent me ahead
> of you to keep you and your families alive and to
> preserve many survivors. So, you see, it was God
> who sent me here, not you! And He is the one who
> made me an adviser to Pharaoh—the manager of
> his entire palace and the governor of all Egypt."
> Genesis 45:5-8

Did you catch that? He recognized that it was GOD who sent him to Egypt. He realized that everything was for a bigger purpose than he could see. He saw that it was God's hand, God's provision that led him down the path he had traveled that brought him to this destiny, and into the plans God had for his life. What if we had Joseph's perspective in the midst of our hardest times, our shattered dreams, our darkened valleys?

Did you know that this is why God's Word is so valuable to us? It shows us story after story to strengthen our faith and encourage us in our walk with God. We watch people in the Bible be transformed through their struggles and it builds our faith as we endure our own. That's why we are to hide His Word in our hearts. That's why it is our sword and a weapon to use in our battles.

Joseph stayed on his caravan, and that Sunday morning in January I decided to stay on mine. It led me to different places, but ultimately it led me to new and glorious places with Him. It led me to places He had laid out for me. It led me to purposes and plans He had ordained for me. It led me to Him.

Psalms 18:16-24 goes hand in hand with the story of Joseph. It goes hand in hand with the story of my life. It goes hand in hand with the story of your life. It's all about how God delivers us from all of our sufferings. How He reaches down and draws us out of many waters. How He delivers us from the strong enemy. How He delivers us because He is pleased with us and He delights in us. The key to that whole passage is what took place in my life that morning. It is what happens in each of our lives if we will allow it.

He makes our life complete when we place all the pieces before Him.

Chapter 4

MAKE ME BIGGER

"My God, my God, why have you abandoned
me? Why are you so far away when I groan for
help? Every day I call to you, my God, but you
do not answer. Every night you hear my voice,
but I find no relief. Yet you are holy..."
Psalm 22:1-3a

SO, HERE I GO. I made the choice. I decided to stay on the
caravan. I let infertility drive me to the place God wanted to
take me all along. It drove me straight to Him.

The battle we are faced with when adversity comes our way
is about trust. It is about faith. It is about our tenacity.

I faced a battle to believe that God is worthy to be trusted
even through hard times. Even though He didn't come through
the way I thought He would or should have. Even though He
didn't change my situation.

We each have to learn what it truly means to come to God
in faith. And here it is: it means coming to Him believing that

He is good, even when life doesn't show it. Even when I can't see proof.

"Faith makes us sure of what we hope for and
gives us proof of what we cannot see."
Hebrews 11:1 CEV

Faith makes us sure of what we hope for. What does that mean? Well, what do we really hope for? We want to know that God loves us. We want to know that He will provide and take care of us. We want to know that He really sees us as His children. We want to know that He cares about our future and that His love for us goes beyond what we can see.

So then, this faith, being sure of what we hope for, is just that. We have faith that He does love us. That He will take care of us. That He is our Father. That He loves us more than our human minds can comprehend. Faith allows our hearts to grab hold of those truths.

Faith gives us proof of what we cannot see. It is faith that sustains us when we can't see the outcomes we hope for. It is faith that sustains us when we can't see our situations changing. It is faith that sustains us when we are surrounded by darkness. Faith not in the fact that He will do anything, but faith in the truth of WHO He is. This is where I found myself journeying straight towards. Because to fully TRUST Him, we have to fully KNOW Him.

Abraham is one of our greatest examples of faith. First, God tells him to leave his homeland and his country and move to a new place that He would show him. He didn't give Abraham the details of the journey up front. He just told Abraham to go. What did Abraham do? He went. Abraham's faith gives us valuable insight into extraordinary faith. The fact that he left as God had directed him without any information was one thing, but his faith when he offered up Isaac was altogether different. Offering up Isaac revealed a faith that would obey without question.

"It was by faith that Abraham offered Isaac
as a sacrifice when God was testing him.
Abraham, who had received God's promises,
was ready to sacrifice his only son, Isaac."
Hebrews 11:17

"Don't you remember that our ancestor Abraham
was shown to be right with God by his actions
when he offered his son Isaac on the altar? You
see, his faith and his actions worked together. His
actions made his faith complete. And so it happened
just as the Scriptures say: "Abraham believed God,
and God counted him as righteous because of his
faith. He was even called the friend of God"
James 2:21-23

Abraham's faith reveals some basic truths about what our faith should look like as well.

Faith will obey exactly as God says.
Faith will obey without question.
Faith will obey regardless of the cost.

Oh, to have a faith that operates like that. In the face of uncertainty, with absolutely no clue if things are going to work out good or bad in the situation, you obey in faith. You do it just as specifically as God as said. You obey without asking any questions. You obey no matter what it costs you. Wow.

I'd love to say I'm there. However, in all honesty, I don't walk in faith like that. There are times when I do, but on a regular, consistent basis? No. I've really been convicted of that a lot lately, too.

Last year God did some amazing things in my life. He taught me some incredible truths and I began to see Him differently than I had before. I learned new traits about Him. All through this, I came to a place where I put my "yes" on the table. I wanted to say yes no matter what He asked of me. For the most part, I did. Well, when it was something I wanted to do anyway.

You see, it's easy to say yes when it's to a calling or a desire we have in our hearts. If God asks us to go to Africa, we say yes, because it's big and it means something. If God asks us to go into full time ministry, we say yes because we see it as significant. But it's not just the big yes that God is after. He's after all the little yeses along the way.

He asks you to walk in forgiveness with someone that you just haven't come to full terms with yet. He asks you to drop your pride and step out and talk to someone or pray for someone. He asks you to do something small, unseen to others, and to step out of the spotlight for a while. He just asks you to take Him at His word, to follow His example, and to live your life accordingly.

Tough questions? Not really. But they require a response from us. They are part of the training process and the means of developing His character within us, so that when the time comes for us to answer His questions that require the big yes, we are ready. We have been training.

It all boils down to obedience. Faith that walks in complete obedience. Period.

As I said before, my days weren't all full of joy after I made the choice to keep going. There were still hard days. I just saw them differently. Instead of them driving me away from God, they drove me to Him. I began to seek Him like I never have. I would sit up late at night in my little glider rocker over in the corner of our living room, and just read and pray. I began to pour myself into an all out pursuit of Him. When I was sad, I would run to Him. When I was happy, I would run to Him. In ALL things, I began to look to Him. I thanked Him for the good days, and I thanked Him for the bad days. I let every part of it draw me to His heart.

One of my favorite verses in the bible is Jeremiah 29:13 and I love how the Message words this scripture:

> "When you come looking for Me, you'll find
> Me. Yes, when you get serious about finding
> Me and want it more than anything else, I'll
> make sure you won't be disappointed."

Seeking God is the key to finding Him. It is the key to overcoming everything in our lives, especially dark valleys. You see, without finding God in the midst of our hard and dark days, without finding Him in the middle of our adversity, we fail to find our source of strength and hope and joy. Whether you believe it or not, it is possible to find joy and peace, hope and contentment in the midst of your pain. But it doesn't come over night. It doesn't come just because you are a Christian. It comes by searching for God in the midst of your storms.

I remember seeing an advertisement one day about the need for adoptive parents of foster children in the Dallas/Fort Worth area. I was intrigued. I was thinking maybe that's what we should do, just go adopt a special needs child from foster care. They were doing a big event one weekend where you could come and learn all about the process and even see videos of children who were ready to be adopted, so we decided to go and check it out.

It was quite overwhelming, to be honest. They had books filled with children in need who were just waiting to be adopted. We watched videos of several children and their stories. It was heartbreaking. Children who had been abandoned at birth. Children who had been severely abused and now suffered extreme mental issues. Children who were born with deformities because of drug and alcohol abuse in the mother. Children who had issues I had never seen. I felt so helpless for them. I wanted them all to find a home. However, as I watched these videos and listened to story after story, I found myself backing away.

I began to realize my heart wasn't ready for something like this. Certainly this couldn't be what God wanted for our lives. To take a child with problems who wasn't even mine? I was so overwhelmed with the thoughts of trying to love a child who didn't belong to me and trying to call them mine. It just didn't make sense to me. I no longer felt a need to adopt.

To be honest, I felt that way because I wanted no part of what I had just seen. I didn't want a child who came from a background like those kids had. I wanted a normal, happy, healthy baby who belonged to me. So I closed the door on this option altogether and decided it was just best to let these thoughts go. It seemed to bring more confusion than ever into my life about the future.

I left that event with a gaping hole in my heart. I had more questions than ever running through my mind. Though I was determined to stay the course and trust God, I was scared of where that would lead me. I didn't want Him to make me adopt a kid I didn't want or love. I didn't understand how people did stuff like that. It's not your flesh and blood. Sure you can love other people's children, but you don't have to claim them as your own. What if you got a child that you didn't really even like after a while? You couldn't just give them back when you got tired of them. Adoption was a forever deal. And I was afraid to do something that would lock me into the unknown. Especially adoption through foster care.

I remember a day in my office at work when it was a not-so-good kind of day. We had been looking at all of our options—adoption, infertility treatments, remain childless, the list goes on. I had so many questions going through my mind. Was He going to perform a miracle and let me get pregnant? Do we just wait on Him to do that miracle? Do we still think about adoption, but just not through foster care? Do we try fertility treatments even if there is just a small chance of it working? Or do we leave it alone and do nothing and live our lives without children? Even still, my biggest question was simple: Why? Why me? Why did I have to go through this? Why, why, why? It's a common question for all of us. And I had been praying and praying about it all. But I was hearing nothing. No direction. No answers. Just silence. That particular morning as I was praying, I begged God to please speak to me about this. I needed to hear His voice and His heart about what we should do. I ended my prayer time, got ready for work and went on my merry way.

I was working at a church and private school during this time. God knew exactly what He was doing when He led me to that position. He knew I would need these people and this place to see me through this time. I was working in the office as a Human Resource Manager. We had a lady in our church, we'll call her "Anna", who would come and pray over every staff person from time to time. It was great. She would come and pray in our offices when we were there and even when we weren't there. This particular day she showed up to pray and I was there. She came into my office and asked if she could just sit and pray while I worked. Of course, I agreed.

My office was like most. I had the nice blue chair sitting in front of my desk for guests. I had the bookshelves filled with pictures and binders and a few of my favorite books. Hanging above my desk was a large framed print of the ocean. It was purely majestic. It had waves rolling in and perfectly set peaceful blue and pink skies behind it. It was just pretty to look at.

Anna came in and knelt down by the blue chair in front of my desk. She did not know all the details of what was going on in my life. She certainly didn't know what I had specifically prayed that morning. So I was anxious to hear what she would pray or hear anything relevant to me personally. I kept working along as she knelt and prayed. I remember she was there for a good while. I was getting curious as to what all she was praying and even more so, I wanted to know what she was hearing!

After what seemed like an eternity, she finally got up off her knees, sat in the blue chair in front of me, and then said, "Do you want to know what He's saying?" I couldn't say yes fast enough. She then proceeded to tell me, "He said, 'I will not speak regarding this situation. You must make Me bigger than the situation.'" She then pointed to the picture hanging above my head behind my desk. She said it was as if I was standing in front of that ocean, but had my back to it. I had no idea what was behind me and how massive it was. I was focused on looking at what was in front of me, but He was so much bigger than that. He was like the majestic ocean behind me that I had not even seen because I was so focused on the other in front of me. I had to change my focus by turning around seeing how big He truly was and trust Him. I had to make Him bigger than my situation.

I was floored at first because she started off in exact response to what I had prayed that morning. I had asked Him to speak. He just told me through her that He was not going to speak regarding my situation. That's about as clear an answer as you can get. Not really the answer I wanted, but it was an answer nonetheless. So the real answer to my prayer was to make Him bigger. To change my perspective.

There we go again…changing our perspective. He already is bigger than anything we face or go through, but His "bigger than" doesn't mean much if we don't apply it. So we have to jump on the wings of faith and let it take us to new heights in Him so that He does become bigger in our eyes. You've heard it said, "Don't tell God how big your mountain is. Tell your mountain how big your God is!" Yet that's exactly what we must do. Make Him bigger than our mountains.

Making Him bigger is really just engaging our faith. It takes faith to make Him more than our problem. But herein lies the key to great victory in our battle. Once He becomes bigger than our problem, our problem no longer has a hold on us. We are set free. As long as our problem is bigger than God, we are bound by fear and uncertainty and our faith is shaken.

Although I may not have really liked the word He spoke that day, I was re-energized that He spoke. I started to make more of Him. He was bigger than the infertility. That's when things began to take another turn spiritually.

I would sit up late at night praying and seeking His face. I came across a song that changed everything, including my perspective. I had become acquainted with Rita Springer and a song she sang called "You Are Still Holy." All I can say is WOW. That song became the anthem of my life.

The song talks about how He is still holy no matter the darkness that surrounds me. It declares that He is still sovereign, even though my times may be confusing. It declares that everything we have, and everything we are belongs completely to Him. And then it acts on those truths by declaring that we dance before Him in the midst of all of it. We come before Him in the midst of our darkness, and we dance. It is absolutely beautiful.

Yeah. That pretty much sums up my life from that point forward! The lyrics are amazing! And they were perfect for my situation. When I heard this song I remember I was lying in the floor in front of the entertainment center in our living room. I had my journal and bible nearby and once those words started resonating in the room, they immediately took ground in my heart. I wrote every word down and haven't stopped singing that song since. It radically transformed me more than I can say.

It was through this song that my heart grabbed hold of a vital truth. He is holy, no matter what the circumstances in my life. He is worthy of my praise, regardless of my situation. And He is altogether GOOD. Period. No matter what my darkness looks like, no matter how devastated I am, no matter how much I understand of what is going on around me, no matter what has happened or is happening, there is one truth that remains solid through it all—He is good; He is holy and He is worthy my praise at all times and in all things. He is worth standing in the midst of my darkest moments and singing praise, dancing in His presence. So I grabbed hold of this truth and I ran with it. As hard and as fast as I could, I ran with it.

It's not an easy process to get to that place in our lives. But it's the place we MUST find in order to survive any storm we encounter and to navigate through the dark valleys. You see, there will always be things that happen to us that will cause worry, or sadness or anger or depression. There will always be distractions that come our way in an attempt to turn our hearts form the only One worthy of our complete focus.

So what do we do? We have to make the conscious choice to move the attention of our hearts away from the situation in front of us, and direct our eyes and our hearts to the One Who walks in on the waves of the storm and says, "It is I. Don't be afraid." We keep our eyes fixed on Jesus and trust that He will guide our ship safely to shore and give us rest.

I love the passage in Isaiah 43:1-2 that gives us such great hope and promise for being tossed about in the storms of life. He gives us the promise and the assurance that when we go through the hard times in our lives, we will not be overcome. So no matter how steep the wave or how heavy the rain or how strong the wind, we will make it through to the other side because of Who is with us.

"When you go through deep waters and great
trouble, I will be with you. When you go through
the rivers of difficulty, you will not drown!"

Isaiah is packed with promises like this one. In chapter 43, verse 19, he tells of providing pathways in the wilderness, rivers in the desert. I love that! It gives me hope that when I find myself in places like that, He provides a path and a means of strength.

I'm glad that we aren't alone in our sufferings. Not just because we have Jesus, Who is there with us, but also, we aren't alone because there are countless others who have endured and they leave us a legacy to follow behind.

One such person is Job. He has meant a great deal to me throughout this process in my life. He endured such pain and hardship. His sufferings were indeed far greater than mine have ever even come close to being. But they are all sufferings just the same. I believe Job paints a picture of what this chapter of my life is all about.

Within one day, Job lost all his oxen, all his donkeys, all his sheep, all his camels, all his children, and all his servants except the four who came to tell him all this news. That's quite a day. Job was a broken man and had good reason to be. Through human eyes, he had every reason to turn his back on God. He had every reason to quit. He had every reason to curse God and just die. But He didn't. He did just the opposite.

Job didn't just set idle through it though. He asked his questions. He asked the question I had been asking throughout my struggles with infertility. He asked why. He really wanted to know why. After all, he was a godly man who loved God and was faithful to him. So, he wanted to know why.

Yet in all these things, Job unlocked the secret that held his freedom through the tragedy. He learned that God was still God, that He was still worthy and holy even in the midst of suffering, and that was all he needed to know. I love the tenacity Job discovers and proclaims through it all. In Job 13:15, he insists, "though He slay me, yet will I praise Him."

Job did it. He found the key to surviving the storm he found himself in. He made God bigger than his issue. He didn't care what came of it, he determined in his heart that he would praise in spite of his circumstances. In essence, Job danced in the face of his darkest moment.

It's amazing to me, though, that even at the end of his story, after his life has been restored, he never got the answer to his question. God never told Job why any of it happened. At the end, Job didn't care anymore. Even before the end, Job resolved in his heart to trust God because of Who God was, not because of what he saw or didn't see Him doing. And God blessed him for it.

There was another time during this that stands out in my memory as well. I mentioned previously that I worked for a church at the time. We were having an off site meeting at my boss's home one morning. I always loved these meetings because while we did talk about work, we also pursued God's heart through prayer. They were always incredible.

This particular time though, will forever be etched into my spirit. We had been in a time of prayer and we were praying over one another. My boss came over and laid her hands on me and began to pray the most powerful prayer I had ever encountered. She began to just talk to God about me and what I was going through. And then she proceeded to ask God to take me on a walk with Him. To lead me into His beautiful gardens and just walk with me. She asked Him to begin to speak to me on this walk. She asked that I would take His hand and let Him begin to pour out His heart over my life and this circumstance. And she ended it by saying that when the walk was over, I would come out of it changed and filled with His heart and wisdom.

A walk. A journey. Grasped hand in hand with my Jesus through the garden of His peace and love. It was like I could literally see in the spirit what she was praying. I could see Him holding out His hand and offering it to me to come away with Him. I could see the gate that we would walk through and enter into the peaceful garden. I could see Him walking along beside me speaking His heart over me. It was beautiful. I could almost smell the flowers along the way.

This was a journey alright. It was a powerful journey that finalized the concept of making Him bigger. It changed my perspective. I left that walk with Him and I felt hemmed in. On all sides, I felt Him surrounding me for the remainder of the journey. He didn't treat me as a woman battling confusion. Instead, He treated me like His daughter, and as a Dad, He wanted to cover me in Him and lead me along the way. And that's exactly what He did.

He led, and I followed.

So here I was, after coming through months and years of heartache, I had found hope based on the truth of Who God was. I felt as though a blinder had been removed from my eyes and I was able to see now that all those lies I had believed about God in the beginning were just to deter me from finding THIS place in Him. Those lies kept me from the freedom I had just stepped into through knowing this.

Regardless of how far in my journey it took me to find these truths, I finally did. And so I set up camp here in my heart. My nights began to be filled with a different song. Instead of weeping and praying for my situation, I began to focus my heart on how good He was, how holy and sovereign He was. Even though I could not see it with my own eyes in my current situation, I proclaimed it over and over every night. I filled my heart with praises instead of questions. I chose to focus my eyes and my heart on Him in all things. A neat thing began to happen as I did. My heart began to see things a little differently than I had. I found a determination in my heart to look at things a new way. I found His gaze and I knew that following His gaze would take me to a different place than I was previously going.

I finally made a decision within me. My questions weren't going to direct me. They weren't going to determine my course. They weren't going to drive me. Rather, my praises would. I laid down my desire to know the answers. I laid down any desire I had to know what He wanted us to do. I gave up the thoughts of adopting. I gave up the thoughts of it all. I wasn't going to pursue any direction in treatment or adoption or anything until I felt He was leading us to do it, but even more, I wasn't going to let my focus be on what the next step was for us, but rather that my focus was on the next truth I could learn of Him. This was my new journey. This was my new goal—to make much of Him. Make Him bigger. Walk with Him. DANCE with Him.

Chapter 5

I Have a Song

"Though the fig tree does not bud and there are no grapes
in the vines, though the olive crop fails and the fields
produce no food; though there are no sheep in the pen
and no cattle in the stalls; YET, will I praise Him. I will
rejoice in the Lord. I will be joyful in God my Savior.
The Sovereign Lord is my strength. He makes my feet like
the feet of a deer; He enables me to go on the heights."
Habakkuk 3:17–19

DURING MY DARKEST TIMES, this verse became a lifeline
to me. I began to see that even in the midst of barrenness,
although it was a different type of barrenness for Habakkuk, he
began to sing in spite of his circumstances. He learned to trust
God in the midst of suffering. He trusted God in the midst of
his trials and for providence, and the Lord gave him sure footed
confidence. He had a song. And I have a song, too.

In the midst of our trials and our sufferings, we have the
choice. We can choose to look only at what's going on around
us. We can look at our losses, our misfortunes, our shattered

hearts, or our betrayals. But God shows us here in His word that we can look higher! In the midst of all these things, we can still rejoice in our Lord. He is our sole source of strength.

Habakkuk didn't always have a song though. His name actually means "to embrace or wrestle." Habakkuk was in a time of wrestling with a difficult issue in his life. If God was good, why was there so much evil going on around him? He was overwhelmed by the devastation that surrounded him. He could not seem to get his focus off the circumstances surrounding him and the bad things happening in his country.

Through his time of grief, though, Habakkuk begins to move from questioning God to trusting God. He moves from worry to worship. He begins with worrying about what's going on around him, but in the end, he ends up worshipping God despite what's going on around him.

We too often get caught up in the lie that questioning God is wrong. The truth is, it's okay to hurt, to cry, to mourn, to grieve and work through our pain. But the fine line here is that we work through it and don't get stuck in it. Habakkuk shows us exactly how we move through that whole process. In the first chapter, we see him in despair. He was low. He was grieving. In chapter two, after he has poured out his heart to God, we see him begin to wait for an answer. Then in chapter three, we see him move into worship. It is here he begins to praise God.

So we see through his life that it IS possible to move from despair to praise. I saw it personally in my life. I continue to see it manifested in my life even today.

After I had grabbed hold of the truth that God was good in spite of my circumstances, I just kept on moving deeper into this journey of discovery; because after all, that's what this whole thing was about so far. It was discovering who He was, and I was determined to go as far and as deep as He'd take me.

I had spent night after night seeking His face and His heart through this. I was slowly noticing my desires change, as well. Before, I had been longing with every part of my being to have a child. I wanted it more than life. While that desire was still there, it was no longer my heart's great desire. You see, during this discovery process, my heart changed so much that I actually found myself no longer thinking about it as much anymore. It just became a "that would be cool if it happened one day" kind of desire. It no longer drove me. It no longer controlled me. I was driven by something far greater than a desire to have a child. I found myself being driven by an overwhelming desire to KNOW Him. I found myself wanting Him more than I ever wanted a child.

People would ask me how things were going and where we were in our process, and I actually started telling people we weren't anywhere in the process. We were still the same place. We had no kids. Couldn't have any kids. Didn't know if we'd ever have kids; yet, I didn't care. I didn't care because the desires of my heart had changed so much that the desire for a baby seemed so small in comparison.

I knew my heart was stronger now and I really felt God had led me to a place of truly letting go of my dream for a baby. One night as I was praying, I felt that I should officially close the door to any grief still in my heart. Instead of leaving an open door to wonder about the what ifs and what-could-have-beens, I buried it. I buried them all. I had my own little "funeral," if you will, and I buried all those desires and questions in the grave and closed it up.

That night I found myself writing a letter. Not to anyone in particular, but to the dream. I wrote to my unborn baby that I would never see or hold. I wrote to the child I would never see grow up. In this letter, I wrote down every thought, every dream I had for a child, what I hoped they would become. I wrote every emotion I had ever felt about the whole process altogether. I said goodbye. This letter was my final stamp. It was the coffin I buried my dream in and then I closed it up and said goodbye. It was my closure. Completely.

Once you bury someone, they aren't coming back. Death is final like that on earth. Once they die, they are gone. You can't go to their grave and dig them up and hope to revive them. No, once they die, they are gone. And once they are in the ground, it's all over. So no matter how bad you want them back, it's impossible for them to come back. When you bury it, it's gone. Period. We have to treat what we bury of the flesh the same way. We can't go back and get it. When it's gone, it's gone. And that's how we have to treat it.

That's what I did that night. The dream was over. It had died. So I did with it what every person has to do when someone they love dies. I laid it in the ground and said goodbye. I couldn't leave any trace of this in my heart. But I didn't just bury my dream in the ground. Instead, I took it to His feet and laid it to rest. I had to say goodbye and I had to leave this death buried at His feet. However, you don't come to His feet standing. I buried this dream and desire and this shattered heart while on my knees.

Something amazing happens at His feet. Something amazing happens when we choose to bury something at His feet. When we go to Him with our death and we are in mourning, and after we have laid it to rest, He does what only He can do. He picks us up, lifts up our heavy hearts and chins with a gentle nudge of His hand, and turns our faces upward. He turns our gaze from what was just buried and He lifts up our heads so that our eyes can see something greater. We see His eyes. In His eyes we find everything. We find hope. We find joy. We find strength. We find all we need. Just like we spoke in previous chapters, we meet His gaze. But His gaze does something different in us after we have buried our pain and shattered hearts at His feet. His gaze then transforms us. And our lives are, well, never the same.

That's what happened that night when I said my final goodbyes to all of those desires and dreams. I looked up and saw His face. That was all I needed from then on. I began to experience, even in greater lengths, the truth to that song I shared with you in the last chapter. I had come into His presence and sat at His feet. I declared with my mouth and my actions that He was holy and He was worthy of my everything.

A few months after this, I had seen where there was a women's conference at Christ For the Nations coming up soon. One of my favorite authors and speakers was going to be there, and I had to go. So I immediately made plans to attend the Friday night portion when she spoke. Little did I know, God was setting me up.

I invited a close friend of mine and we went together. The night started off wonderful. Beautiful worship and just a sweet presence of the Lord had filled the place. The speaker got up to speak and was sharing about holiness. It was good. I was taking notes as fast as I could write. In the middle of her message, from out of nowhere, she began to say some things that floored me and nearly made me fall out of my chair.

Her message was on holiness, but here in the middle she stopped and she proceeded to talk about Isaiah 54:1, which says, "Rejoice Oh barren woman, rejoice you who have never born a child." She then went on to say, "God is asking the barren woman to dance before Him. He is asking the woman who is walking through adversity to come and dance before Him even in the midst of her despair. In the midst of her darkness, He is asking her to dance before Him. The woman who has no child, He is asking her to come before Him and dance. To dance in the face of her deepest pain. In the middle of being surrounded by nothing but pure darkness, He is asking her to come and dance before Him through it." I couldn't believe what I had just heard. I dropped my pin I was so blown away. I couldn't even process all that she had just said. What made it so profound is that this is the place I had already found myself navigating toward in my journey. I had been surrounded by the darkness of despair, of shattered dreams, and I had found my way into His chambers. Now He was speaking through this woman, telling me what to do when I got into His presence. He was telling me to dance.

After the speaker talked about what she had just said a little more, she interrupted her message even further and did an altar call in the middle. She asked for every woman who was barren in her womb to come forward and kneel before God at the altar. Scores of women flooded the altar. I was in disbelief. Of course I had made my way as fast as I could down to that altar. All these women, here at the altar, kneeling before God and pouring out their hearts to Him. It was beautiful. She began to pray over all of us. She prayed that God would touch our wombs and make us fertile, in whatever way He chose to do so.

An interesting thing was happening in my heart though as she prayed. I found myself thinking that I didn't want Him to open up my womb and give me children right now. I was loving the place I had found at His feet and I didn't want Him answering my prayer to cause me to leave. Not until He had done everything in me that He wanted to do in this process. I know, it sounds crazy. But I had just seen Him so strong through these last few months I wasn't ready to let go of it. Not that by Him answering my prayers would I have to let go of Him, but right now, those desires had drove me to Him and I was determined I wasn't going to let go until He was done with His work in me.

We left the altar and went back to our seats. My friend was just as dumbfounded as I was at what had just happened. We had a glorious chat on the way home about how amazing the night had been and how God had spoken so specifically about everything going on in my life. It was a night I'll never forget. That's for sure.

That night was so vital to everything. That night became the song of my life. That night became the title of this book. I was learning first hand what it meant to dance in the dark. So I began this phase of my journey. I learned to dance in my darkness. I learned how to offer up praises in the darkest of nights. When my heart hurt the worst, I would sing and I would dance in the presence of my Beloved.

The best part is that when you start dancing in your darkness, you start dancing on all of your graves. So those things I buried at His feet? I was beginning to dance over them now. I was dancing on the grave of the hurts I had buried. I was dancing on the grave of a shattered heart, a shattered dream, and a desire to have anything other than Him. Let me just tell you, once you are to the place where you are dancing on your graves, worship is transformed in your life. It takes on a whole new meaning. It becomes even more personal, more real.

I have found this is what God desires of all us. He wants us to get to the point where we are able to dance before Him and celebrate His goodness in spite of our circumstances. He wants us to be able to celebrate Him for who He is, even when our circumstances don't give us a reason to celebrate.

This is how we find joy in the mourning. Taking our eyes off us and our desires and placing our full attention, all of our worship, all of our praise, on the One who is truly worthy of our praise above all other things.

Can you picture it? A grief stricken, anguished woman. She has no reason to smile or laugh, let alone sing and dance. Here she is, surrounded by complete darkness. She's dancing before a God she may not fully understand, but One that she fully loves because she has come to know the love that He has for her. With arms stretched out in complete abandon, with head held high, with eyes focused on Him, she begins to dance and twirl and sing with everything inside of her. She celebrates His majesty, she celebrates His holiness, and she celebrates Him, regardless of her own disappointments.

A barren woman with a broken heart has no reason to celebrate in the natural. She has experienced the never ending cycle of grief and disappointment so much that her candle has been dimmed and her hopes crushed beneath it all. So as this barren woman comes dancing before God, celebrating Who He is in spite of her circumstances, when her circumstances give her no reason to celebrate at all, she is offering a sacrifice of praise. She has allowed God to take the ashes of her life and turn them into something beautiful: a heart full of worship for her King. She has forsaken all else. She has laid down her pain, her disappointments and her dreams. She has placed them all at His feet as she completely gives herself in worship to Him.

Can we say that we love Him more than what we are praying for? Can we say that we love Him even if He never answers our prayers? Can we say that He is good, even when our circumstances are not? Can we take our deepest hurts and fears and bury them beneath His feet? How beautiful that must be in the eyes of Father. I can only imagine what it does to Him when He sees a broken individual offering praise. Or when someone takes all they have and pours it out on Him.

One of the most beautiful stories in the bible is the woman who poured the perfume on Him. It's the story of Mary and her alabaster box. Her worship still echoes into our lives today. It was so powerful because it cost her something of great value. It cost her everything. She spent all she had at the feet of Jesus. She discovered that He is worth giving up everything we hold dear. It was a worship that cost her something. That's a worship that touches Father's heart.

Mary radically cut away all that the world thought was valuable. She wanted to waste her life at Jesus' feet. She was radical in her worship, and it was beautiful in His eyes. You see, we can't give God our lives when we get to heaven. We can only do that here on earth. There will be no tears in heaven, so when we offer up worship through our tears on earth, think of how valuable that is to God. It grabs hold of His heart.

Mary found the treasure of His heart and she knew it was something worth losing everything for. Have we found the treasure of His heart yet? If so, are we willing to pour out everything we have in order to give our worship back to Him?

I don't know about you, but I want a holy embrace to define my life. What the world sees as a waste, I want to pour over His feet. He IS someone worth giving up everything for. And He is worth our fragrant offerings.

Anybody can dance and sing when life is good. It's easy to offer praises when our lives are going just like we had planned. Anybody can sing when they are being abundantly blessed. It's easy to sing when things are smooth sailing. But "worship" happens when we dance in the face of adversity, when we offer praises to a God who hasn't answered our prayers. Worship is praising Him like He's already answered you, even when He hasn't.

Contrary to popular belief, worship is not standing in church and singing a song with our lips. Worship is singing our songs to God even when our lives don't show we have a reason to be singing. It's choosing to dance before Him when we are surrounded by only darkness. It's throwing our hands back in complete abandonment and saying that He is holy, He alone is our reason to sing, and He is GOOD-regardless of what our current situations tell us. He asks us to sing in our barren times (Isaiah 54:1), to find our hope and our joy only in Him. Why? Because He knows that when we find our hearts deepest longings and all we truly need in HIM, we will no longer be driven by the temporal, but our hearts and lives will be focused on and engaged in what is of eternal value.

Another song that meant a lot to me was again by Rita Springer. It's titled "Worth It All." It basically says that regardless of what we go through, He is worth the struggles. It's worth what we find at the end. That's what dancing in the darkness represents. It's making a statement with our lives that He is worth every tear, He is worth every heartbreak, because they draw us to Him and we find HIS heart through it all.

It was great to be free from something that had such a hold on me. It was great to just not care what happened with any of it. I no longer cared if we adopted. I no longer cared what happened. All I knew was that I had found Jesus, and He was all I needed.

Sometimes it takes going through difficult times to find our songs. Sometimes it takes being surrounded in darkness to find our Source of light. Sometimes it takes dancing on our graves to find new life in its place.

Chapter 6

TIMING IS EVERYTHING

"But I trusted in, relied on, and was
confident in You, O Lord; I said, You are
my God, my times are in Your hands."
Psalm 34:14-15

IT OCCURS TO ALL of us. It comes and goes with each tick of the clock. You can't stop it, you can't turn it back. Once it's over, it's over. It is as faithful as the rising and setting of the sun. Depending upon where you are, it can be different for you than others. You may be ahead; you may be behind depending on your location. It shows no favoritism for one person to the next. It just "is" and always will be. TIME.

How many times a day do you or someone else ask the same question, "What time is it?" Time has always been around, but our means of tracking it and deciphering have developed since its inception. In ancient times it was measured by the sun and seasons. Today we measure it by time zones. Time is important. We run our lives by it. Everything revolves around time.

As important as time is to us, it is even more important to God. The Greek New Testament alludes to time in different ways. One such word used frequently is "chronos" from which we get the word "chronological." This is the kind of time we are most associated and familiar with. It refers to the ticking of the clock. It is the movement of days on a calendar. It is time on the move. It refers to duration and length of time.

There's another word for time used in the bible as well. It's called "kairos" and it is a term used to describe the right or opportune time. It is described as an opening, or a time when conditions are right for the accomplishment of a crucial action. It can be a fraction of a moment. It can happen in a flash or it can take longer. It is a special selected period of Divine determination. It operates within a human time, but it is the focus on fulfillment of God's ultimate purposes.

God created time, and in His sovereign kairos time He interacts and enters into our chronos time all according to His perfect will and His plans. He brings about the perfect alignment of natural and supernatural forces that creates an environment for a specific opening to occur. Kairos is a time when heaven touches earth. It is a time of heaven's visitation to our lives.

The key to kairos moments lies not in the fact that they are presented to us, but in the fact that they must be seized. They must be seized in order to achieve their purposes in our lives. I believe that it also involves seizing Father's heart through these times.

Kairos is a time when your name is called. How you respond determines everything. Hell lives in fear of your kairos moments. Our enemy knows that when kairos moments show up, incredible things begin to happen.

The Bible is filled with kairos moments. Some were seized, some were not. Peter was in the boat in the middle of a storm. He saw Jesus out in the middle of it, standing on the water. Jesus bids Peter to come to Him. He told Peter to get out of the boat and come to Him. Kairos moment for Peter. If he goes, he risks failure, he risks drowning. But if he stays, he risks missing out on one of the most defining moments of faith in his life. What does Peter do? He seizes the moment and says yes. He was given a moment that required immediate action. It required a response. Peter answered yes.

David had a kairos moment. He had been out tending sheep for his father. His brothers were all part of Saul's army and they had gone out to fight the Philistines. David went to their camp and heard Goliath shouting words against his God. No one would go out and face Goliath. Until now. This little shepherd boy was presented with a kairos moment and what did David do? He seized it. He said yes. He took a slingshot and fist full of rocks to go out and defeat his enemy. What does God do? He gives David the victory. Amazingly, David slays Goliath with a single shot.

I had a kairos moment. I've had a few throughout this process, actually. I had a moment when I was given the opportunity to keep going or give up. I could quit the race altogether, get off the caravan or stay on the journey and trust God with blind faith. I seized the moment and said yes. The outcome? I learned how to worship despite my circumstances and I found the Fathers heart.

I had a moment that morning in my office when my friend told me to make God bigger. I could've said no and continued to keep my focus on the wrong thing. Or I could say yes and discover that perspective changes everything. It determines how far and how high I can fly with Him. I said yes.

One of the most substantial moments came, though, several months after that night at Christ For The Nations. I had let go of any plans I had. My husband and I didn't care what the future held in terms of us having children any longer. We were both content with where we were, and we knew that God's hand was guiding us through it all anyway. My husband processed things much differently than I did, but in the end, we both met at the same place.

It was during the spring of 2003, when some of our friends told us they were going to begin the foster parent classes through a local Christian home. It's funny, because just months earlier I had said this was something I could never do. I had no desire. Yet, listening to my friends speak about it, I found my heart stirred. The classes had already started, but were still early enough that we could join. We went home that day and talked about it. After praying, we both felt that we should give this a try. All we knew at the moment was that we felt God leading us to foster. We figured we were just meant to be the passing through homes for kids who needed a chance while they were either waiting to be adopted or waiting on their birth parents to get their acts together and regain custody of their children. We thought no further than that at the beginning. So we made the necessary phone calls and got signed up and started our classes.

It has always amazed me that any teenager on drugs, or on the streets, or a high school kid who just went too far in a relationship can get pregnant, and it's no big deal. Yet, here we were, good, upstanding Christian people who had to go through the ringer in order to become parents of the children that these young kids had or situations similar. Kind of funny actually.

Nevertheless, here we were. It's no easy task to become a foster parent. You don't just sign up and say "give me some kids." Quite the contrary. It is a detailed process that involves tons of paperwork, hours of classes on specific topics related to children and special needs kids and an in depth review of your life, your marriage and your home.

I can still remember there were times during the classes where I thought we might be a little crazy for doing this. They would present stories of situations and the things you had to do. They would teach us how to defend ourselves against violent children. It was a little frightening, to say the least.

As the process went on, we found ourselves feeling drawn to do more than just foster. Our hearts began to turn to adoption. And not just any adoption, it was being turned toward these children we would meet through foster care.

Now, one of the big things with foster care is that you are not guaranteed to be able to adopt any child that is placed in your custody. It is a vigorous and detailed process to find children who are ready to be adopted. A lot of the children that come through do end up getting placed back with their parents or with a blood relative. So you have to go in to the process knowing that you can't let yourself get attached to a child because it's very probable you will be giving that child back.

The classes had really begun to set in on me emotionally. I was overwhelmed at what some of these children had to endure in their lives. I was a little scared at what we would encounter when we had a placement. My mind started to have a lot of questions. I began to become unsure if we had actually heard God's voice to do this. Nothing seemed clear. I was lost.

It was a Friday morning in June when God spoke to me loud and clear about this. He gave me His heart and shed light on everything we were doing.

We were having another off campus work meeting at IHOP that morning. I had gotten there early and decided to just sit in my car and read my bible as I waited for the rest of the group. Little did I know I was about to be met with a clear word from God.

I had flipped open the bible to Isaiah and just asked God to speak to me as I poured over His Word. He knew what was in my heart. He knew I was questioning what we were doing with all of this foster care process. I just needed to know if we were on the right path.

I ended up in Isaiah 49. Can I just say that nothing has been the same since?

I started reading from verse one. With each verse it seemed He was making His truth and ways known. I had been specifically asking Him to confirm things to me about us pursuing foster care and adoption through foster care. I just wanted to make sure we were clearly hearing His voice. Let me just tell you, He answered me loud and clear that Friday morning.

The chapter specifically spoke of God answering in due time, at the right time. It specifically spoke of being given children in a barren land. My translation even specifically said the phrase "foster father". Now to you, that may be circumstantial. You may think none of that has anything to do with what I was praying. But to me, that chapter was as if God Himself came and sat down in the car with me that day and began speaking. I felt completely at peace with what we were doing. I knew we were on the right path, at the right time, and that God was leading the way.

During our classes, we had the opportunity to do a weekend respite care for another foster family who had children they were fostering, but this couple needed to go out of town. We were chosen to fill in that weekend and keep the two children. I had met these kids before and already loved them. I knew their background and the situation they came from. I knew it was a possibility they could be adoptable soon. And I have to be honest—I was trying to take a few steps ahead of what I saw and go down the "what if" road with these two kids. Bad mistake.

The one thing you have to go into any fostering situation with is that you will more than likely be giving these kids back at some point. After all, the ultimate goal is to reunite the children with their parents if at all possible and the state does counseling and all sorts of things to try and help the parents of these children. But as much as you tell yourself you probably aren't going to be keeping these kids, emotions do have a way of setting in.

I loved every minute of our weekend with this sweet brother and sister. They both had some issues they were dealing with, but I just fell in love with them. I loved having children in my home that I got to care for and treat like they were my own. It felt good to finally feel like a mommy. I loved putting them to bed at night and waking them up in the morning. I loved fixing meals for them to eat. Everything felt right except for one important thing—they weren't mine.

The weekend ended and we had to take the children back to the family who had custody of them at the time. It was so incredibly hard. I held back my tears as long as I could when we said our goodbyes, but once I made it to the car, the floodgates opened. I knew all along I'd be giving them back, but somewhere deep within me I still had the hope that maybe…just maybe…these could be mine.

As much as I wanted to call them my own, they belonged to someone else. And so after shedding a few tears of heartache, I had to release it back to God and walk in trust that this was not my plan to fulfill, but His. So I trusted in the fact that He knew exactly where I was. He knew all the days laid out for me and He had a plan. He would let me in on the details as I needed to know. I trusted in the fact that I was in the palm of His hands, and that my times were, indeed, in His hands.

In August we finished up our classes. It had been a fun journey. The classes themselves were great and enlightening, but the home study was even more fun. The final stamp on your approval comes after a completed home study.

A home study wasn't at all what I thought it would be to begin with. You answer tons of questions about you, your childhood, your life, your marriage…everything. Both you and your spouse do this. Then they come to your home and do a lot of the same thing. Asking questions, learning who you are. It's a bit overwhelming, but in the end, I understand why they do it. These kids have already gone through enough turmoil in their lives. They want families that can help them and be a good fit. So I knew it was all for a good purpose.

After everything was finalized, my husband went by the offices to pick up our official license that showed we were approved to be foster parents. If memory serves me correct, I believe it was a Friday in late August. I wasn't able to go, so he went and did it for us.

I was on my way home from work when I got a phone call from him. He proceeded to tell me how he had picked up our license and they had pulled him into an office to ask him about a potential placement. The first question they asked was, "So, how many kids would you be willing to take?" My husband's response, "Well, how many are we talking?" He wasn't sure if we were about to get a dozen or two, but was curious at this point.

The caseworker then told him about three brothers that were in need of a home. They had been in foster care for some time. The parental rights had already been terminated, so they were eligible to be adopted after the six month period of fostering. However, they had actually already had one failed adoption. So these kids had been through a lot. Now we had to make a decision.

I had always thought I'd like about two kids. Preferably a boy and a girl. You know, get the best of both worlds. Never really thought about more than two. But, I was open and thought God might be having a sense of humor with this now.

It was weird, this whole thing. It was like as soon as he told me about it all, I felt in my spirit that these were my boys. I didn't have to see a picture. I just knew. I didn't care that "my" plans of two kids and a boy and a girl weren't in the picture. I just knew that my heart was saying yes as loud as it could. And I didn't even know their stories yet.

After I told my husband I felt we should do this, he told me he had gotten the same thing. Then he did it. He showed me the picture. It was at that moment that life as I know it completely stopped for a moment in time. I saw those faces and it was like I just gave birth. These were MY children. These were MY answered prayers for so many years. I was looking at the three most beautiful boys I had ever laid eyes upon.

At the time, they were seven years, two years, and nineteen months old. They had been in foster care for almost two years. I can't go into complete details of their history, but they had suffered abuse and neglect. It's hard to imagine all they endured in their short lives. The abuse and neglect is one thing, but to be ripped away from your home and your family is just inconceivable to me. It breaks my heart.

After we said yes, the process started. There actually came a question about them allowing all three boys to be placed together. They underwent psychological evaluations and sessions to determine if this was in the best interest of the boys. My faith was being tested yet again.

I had already determined in my heart that all three of these boys were mine. I didn't care what doctors and therapists said, they were meant to be mine. But as the weeks progressed, I have to admit, my faith got a little shaky.

I remember coming down the interstate one day and the song by Mercy Me, "Word of God Speak," was on the radio. I was listening to the words of it and thinking back on some things that had happened at work that day. God just began speaking to my heart about how He had specifically taken care of things for me at work that day. Not even big things. They were little things. Like, for instance, I was craving a mini snickers bar so bad. Nobody seemed to have any that usually did. I made it into the office of one last person who, at first, thought they didn't have one either. But then, out of nowhere, he finds one in the bottom of his jar. It was just a little God-wink.

A few other things happened like that earlier in the day. As I was listening to this song, God began to speak to me and show me how much He cares for me by reminding me of all the little things He did that day. It wasn't earth shattering things. It was little things that you do for someone you love. He began showing me that if He cares about the little details in my life, how much more does He care about the big details of my life? Then He began to show me that as much as I care about these boys, whom I had never even met yet, how much more did HE care about them and their future? He filled my heart with peace that this was in HIS hands, not the courts. That settled it in my heart. I would just wait until things came to be.

We got the call towards the end of September that the courts had approved them all three to be placed together. I was at a retreat for work when Ronnie called to tell me the news. His words when I answered the phone, "We got the boys. They are all ours!" I immediately stood up and shouted it to the whole room!

I can't even begin to tell you what happened in my heart at that moment. I believe hearing those words was even better than hearing "you're pregnant." It was like all of the failed pregnancy tests and monthly let downs and emotional roller coasters all came back—but this time, they were overtaken by the absolute joy of hearing that I was about to become a mother. Yet, not just any mother. I was becoming a mother of three boys, whom God had created just for me.

My dream was about to be fulfilled. I had stayed on the caravan. It led me to here. It led me to my dream. It led me to my destiny. I was about to hear someone call me the word I had always longed to hear....MOM.

This was the greatest kairos moment I could've asked for! But the neat thing is that this was really more of a kairos season than a single moment. You see, God had me in a time of preparation for this one moment, but it was during the season that I was given so many opportunities to make me ready for this specific time. All of my yeses that I gave God along the way prepared me for the big yes that was yet to come. Who knows what life would have looked like had I chosen to make the jump at the beginning and turn my back on God. I don't even want to know. I'm so thankful He was patient with me through the process and allowed me time to find my way into His arms. I'm glad He loved me enough to give me grace. I'm glad He had a plan, even when I couldn't see it. He changed my perspective on the issue, and then surprised me with the ending I wasn't expecting. He's just cool like that. And it's one reason I just love him so.

Kairos....when He interacts and enters into our chronos time all according to His perfect will and His plans. He brings about the perfect alignment of natural and supernatural forces that create an environment for a specific opening to occur. Kairos is a time when heaven touches earth. It is a time of heaven's visitation to our lives.

Heaven had indeed touched earth. He had indeed interacted and entered into my world according to a perfect and divine plan. It was His timing. It was His moment. It was my kairos.

Chapter 7

HE IS FAITHFUL

"So don't worry about these things, saying, 'What will
we eat? What will we drink? What will we wear?'
These things dominate the thoughts of unbelievers,
but your heavenly Father already knows all your needs.
Seek the Kingdom of God above all else, and live
righteously, and he will give you everything you need."
Matthew 6:33

I LOVE THAT GOD writes our stories and just lets us see a
page at a time. Now, my curiosity and impatient self doesn't
necessarily love it, but my heart knows that I couldn't handle
seeing more than one page at a time. The way He writes a story
just blows my mind.

I love the story He is writing in my life and my family's
life.

After we got word that things were going to happen,
that we were going to get the boys, I cannot even begin
to explain in words what was happening within my spirit.

Turning the page in the story of my life and reading THAT just confirmed even more that trusting Him was the greatest thing I could do.

Once things were finalized with the courts and the paperwork was completed, the next journey of our lives was set into motion. Our first meeting with the boys was set up, and the plan was put in place to give us full custody.

I'll never forget talking with our caseworker and learning things about them. She had given us a few pictures of them and I displayed them in my office like the proud parent to be that I was. I wanted to know everything. Looking at their pictures just made me fall in love with them even more. And knowing that very soon, these three beautiful children were going to be mine, well, it was more than my heart could imagine.

One of the projects we had to do was to make a scrapbook of our lives so that at our first meeting we could give it to the boys and they would have it until they got officially placed in our home. This is how we would introduce them to our families, and to our home.

Prior to us meeting the boys, we had to get our house ready for their arrival. We had gone and bought beds and had gotten their rooms all complete. But that was nothing. My amazing church family threw me a baby shower.

Remember the stories of how baby showers broke my heart? Well, my Father redeemed that for me when He used my friends to bless my socks off with the one they gave me.

They did the shower at our house and it was beyond words. My home was filled with all the people who had prayed for me and with me during the darkest time of my life. Instead of wiping my tears of sorrow, they were celebrating God's faithfulness to me and to their prayers. It was beautiful. I can't imagine anyone having a more beautiful baby shower than the one I was experiencing that night.

My dining room was packed with gifts. They had all written encouraging words for me and tips on being a mom. They prayed over me and blessed my home and our family. My home was transformed and it was all I could do to contain myself. I love the family of God and how my sisters in Christ carried me through some rough days, and now, they were celebrating with me. The best part was that Christ was receiving all the glory for the great things He had done.

Our first official meeting with the boys was finally set. It was set up at the foster home where they were currently staying. Our caseworker met us there so she could observe and see how things went. I'll never forget that day as long as I live.

We pulled up into the yard of the home and they all came outside to meet us. I can still remember the oldest, Jeremiah, coming over and giving me a hug. He came up just a little above my waist and he was the most beautiful seven year old I had ever laid eyes on. Next we met Charlie and Taylor. Right off the bat they were smiling. Taylor was a chubby little nineteen month old with a head of red hair and a smile that made the world disappear. Charlie stole my heart with his big eyes and a smile that I could almost hear my heavenly Father saying "welcome home" through. I was almost overwhelmed as I looked into their faces and saw the last several years and all the heartaches and heartbreaks and all the tears come to the end of that chapter. I was seeing a new story unfold. I was seeing grace and redemption first hand. I was seeing restoration of what had been taken from me. I was seeing Jesus in the faces of these children.

We went inside so we could spend some time with the children and interact with them. Jeremiah made his way over to the kitchen table where he wanted to show me he could count up to one hundred. We played a game of who could count the fastest. Charlie sat in the floor with Ronnie and proceeded to line all of his little matchbox cars up in a neat, straight line, all according to the color of the car. He had them in perfect order. Taylor sat and observed everything. On occasion, he would give you a smile if you caught his eye. Man, I love that kid!

After some time we went outside to play. Jeremiah loved to play baseball and basketball so we did some of that together. I'll never forget being outside and Charlie was playing close by me and I heard him saying a word that didn't register with me until the caseworker said, "He's talking to YOU, Stacy." He had been saying a word I had always longed to hear, but being referred to as this word had not registered in my mind yet. What was he saying to me? He was calling me....MOMMY.

I have to say, I was overwhelmed. No one had ever called me that. I had longed so desperately to hear it for so many years. Now, here I was, meeting the three children who would soon be mine and on the first meeting my sweet Charlie was calling me his mommy. What a gift.

We continued to play outside for a bit until it was time to pack up and go. I didn't want to leave. I wanted to take them with me. They were so beautiful. I couldn't wait for them to officially be mine.

We set up the next few weeks of meetings with them, so that the next time we would take them to get ice cream or something with just us, and then we'd do a weekend with them and then they would come home with us for good. They were trying to ease the children into it, let them get acquainted with us and then make the transition.

Before we left that day, we all got together and took our first official family photo. I still have it proudly displayed on my desk. I look at it all the time and it never fails, I can go back to that exact day of that first meeting as if it happened yesterday. One of the most precious moments in my life.

On our next visit we all five went to eat at Dairy Queen together. I remember getting to their house and trying to figure out the car seats and then getting Charlie and Taylor strapped in. Ronnie and I had no practice at this so it was always an adventure to say the least. Our afternoon was wonderful. Just eating ice cream and getting to know each other.

The next weekend we got to have a weekend stay with them. We went and picked them up on a Friday and they were able to stay with us all weekend and we took them back to the foster parents on Sunday.

I will have to say, the weekend visit was amazing. Having them in my house was nothing short of divine. I loved everything about them. But they all seemed to carry one trait that was noticeable to anyone they came in contact with: they all had these amazing smiles that you couldn't tear your eyes away from. Their smiles melted your heart and took you to a happy place. Their smiles made my heart feel at home.

That Sunday morning was wonderful taking them to church for the first time. I held my head high as I walked through those doors with Taylor on my hip, Ronnie was carrying Charlie and Jeremiah was in between us all. Here we were, for the first time, a glimpse at what our family was going to look like. It was perfect.

I wasn't really excited about taking the boys back to their foster home that afternoon. I was ready for this to be complete so our family would be together.

Our official placement took place on October 31st. So, while everyone else was excited about Halloween, I was celebrating our "gotcha day" with our boys! We picked them up that day and got all of their belongings and headed home. OUR home. No more visits. No more taking them back. They were officially in our custody. It was a beautiful day.

I fixed a quick dinner that night and we got all dressed up to go to our church event. That night was perfect. It was our first official night out as legal guardians of the boys, and we got to treat them like they were ours. I enjoyed all of the joys I had longed for. We stood in line for games. We did the hayride. We ate junk food. We laughed. It was everything I had hoped for and so much more.

The next six months seemed to go by pretty fast. We had some great times and first memories along the way. All of our family made trips out to see us and meet the boys. It was great. The boys took up with everyone like they had known them all along. I couldn't have asked for a better transition.

Christmas is probably the greatest and most memorable time for us. We had our first official family portrait done in December. It was an experience to say the least! It was on a Saturday morning. We spent the allotted hour there trying to get everyone looking and smiling at the same time. You know, all the great stresses of family portraits. And then for some reason, we decided to take the boys to see Santa that night at the mall and get their picture made with him, too. I have to say, it's the greatest Santa picture ever. Charlie and Taylor hated him! The picture shows it, too. I love it. It was a great memory. But the greatest Christmas memory would have to be Christmas itself.

Now, most of you are probably thinking it is some great sentimental moment we had sharing our first Christmas together. While that is true and it was great, the moment is not what you think it is.

It was Christmas Eve and Ronnie and I had planned to make a big meal and start our own family tradition. So we grilled some steaks and made all kinds of goodies. It was a delicious meal. The boys all ate and did great. Charlie, however, started a downward decline from that point.

As the night progressed, he seemed to start feeling bad. He had just been lying around some on the couch, but we had just chalked it up to him being tired from all we had done that day. We put them to bed a little early so "Santa" could make his way there, and went on about our business.

About two hours later as we were getting the living room all set up with Santa, we heard Charlie crying. I went in to get him and he was burning up with a fever. Now, this was our first "health" issue, and we were newbies. Needless to say, it didn't make for a great combination.

We did what every parent who has a child with a fever does—we put him in a cold tub of bathwater! Poor guy, I'm sure that was pleasant for him. Then we gave him some popsicles and juice. You know, using all the tricks to getting rid of fever. ☺

We were sitting in the floor in our bedroom and I had him laid up in my lap. I was just holding him trying to make him feel better, not knowing what on earth we were doing. I was enjoying being this loving mom when all of a sudden, I hear an eruption coming forth from Charlie's mouth, which was followed by every single piece of food he had eaten that day. And it was now all over me. From head to toe. Ronnie came in and quickly turned away at the smell.

To this day I don't know how I didn't join in with Charlie because I don't do well with that smell. I can only chalk it up to the grace of God covering my nose so I could tend to him instead of joining in the fun myself. After getting him all taken care of and cleaned up and feeling better, we of course titled our first Christmas as "Christmas Heave." And poor Charlie will never live that one down!

Being a first time mom also presented itself with some interesting challenges for me. I wasn't used to taking more than one person with me anywhere. So, naturally, I never thought of diaper bags, and sippy cups and things like that. I would proudly drop the two younger ones off at the nursery at church only to be met with questions such as, "Did you bring their sippy cups?", or "Do you have your extra diapers?", or "Did you bring a diaper bag?" Yeah, I officially felt like a loser! But they were always full of grace and helped me out. Thank God!

Trips out to the mall and Wal-Mart were just the same. I never remembered to bring anything. I am so scatterbrained as it is, but man, throw in three other people I now have to look out for and you have brought on complete chaos in my head! I wouldn't change it for anything. Those days were priceless and completely perfect in every way. Even the trips to the doctor where they would ask me if the blue card was up-to-date, and to which I would proudly answer, "What's a blue card?", followed by a brief explanation of why I didn't know the answer. Yeah, that's me. Mom of the year. But I was a happy mom, that's for sure.

The months went by and finally, after all the waiting, May 7th arrived. Our adoption had been set for Friday, May 7th.

The end was near. We were about to officially and legally become the adoptive parents of the three greatest kids in the world. I was about to officially be declared a mother.

It worked out that my parents and Ronnie's mom were able to come in for the adoption ceremony. We started out the morning at the courtroom. I'll never forget the emotions that were racing through my heart and the thoughts traveling through my mind. This day had finally arrived. I was about to legally become a mother. My heartaches were over. My life was complete.

The court liaison called our name into the courtroom after what seemed like an eternity. We took our seats and waited on the judge to then call our case. It was so exciting awaiting our turn at the "bench" before the judge. I guess I kind of looked at this like my delivery. This was my hospital room, the judge was my physician, and I was about to "give birth" and become a mother. Yeah, it was a little different than most women go through. My pregnancy had been different altogether. Most women go through nine months. I had gone through nearly seven years. Most women conceive and get pregnant naturally. I had conceived these babies on my knees, on my face before God through many tears and heartaches. Yet, when all is said and done, we are all mothers just the same. I kind of like how that worked.

We finally found our turn in front of the judge. He went through a series of questions for us and after a few moments of his speaking, he proclaimed us a family. There it was. My dream. My hearts cry for so many years. It all came to a conclusion on this day. It was official. Ron and Stacy Fulton were now the proud parents of Jeremiah, Charlie and Taylor. We were a family. My heart was complete.

Immediately after the court process was finalized, we made our way to the agency that we did the adoption through for an adoption ceremony. Our entire family, along with my parents and Ronnie's mom were there. A guest speaker gave a short message, and then they had all of us come forward and light candles. We lit candles for each of our children that had found their forever home. Then my parents and Ronnie's mom lit a candle for other children still waiting to be adopted. At the end, they presented our adoption leaf that went up on the adoption wall. Each of the boys had one. It had their name, who they were adopted by and the date. It was perfect. The whole day was just perfect.

That took place on Friday. Guess what was Sunday of that same weekend? Mothers Day. Yes, Mothers Day was just two days after our adoption. God had orchestrated the whole thing so that on the weekend of our adoption being finalized, I would get to celebrate my first Mothers Day. I mean, how much more perfect could it be? I couldn't have written a story this great if I had tried!.

The weekend was amazing. That Sunday we celebrated my becoming a mom. Not only did I get to enjoy my first Mother's Days as an official mom, but I also got another sweet surprise. Our church always did gifts for things such as "oldest mom", "youngest mom", "mom with most kids", etc… As our Pastors wife was calling out the different categories, she came to the one that got me. She called for the "newest mom." Needless to say, I had been an official mom for two days, so guess who won that? Yep, me. That moment was priceless.

Our pastor was also sweet enough to allow us to do our dedication of the boys since we had family in from out of town. So, on the day that broke my heart for so many years, God redeemed it in one instant. He declared me a mother, and on that day, we gave the gifts He had given us back to Him. The three beautiful boys He had placed in our care, and put in our hands, we then raised back up to Him and declared them as not ours, but belonging to Him. It was the perfect ending to the perfect weekend. It was the perfect ending to this particular journey. It was a fairytale if I've ever seen one. And it was mine. This was my life.

I've seen redemption before. I've watched God turn lives that were headed for destruction into something beautiful. I've seen God answer prayers for people. I've seen Him do some amazing and incredible things—for other people. Now, I've seen Him do some great things in my life, too, don't get me wrong. He took my desolate and dark soul and brought me to life when He saved me. He turned my life completely around and put me on a different path. He restored my soul and truly lifted me from a miry pit. He provided a glorious salvation for me.

But I had never seen Him do so many incredible things like I saw Him do during this process in our lives. Especially the way He brought it all together. It was absolutely perfect. I mean perfect. I wouldn't change a thing.

I learned a lot through the fostering process with the boys. I learned that parenting was a lot more than I had ever thought. It was tough! But so very rewarding in so many ways. I began to see that each of us are no different than these kids. We all are in need of acceptance and a family. We are all in need of someone to give us a second chance at life. Even beyond that, some of us just need a chance because the situations we find ourselves in have taken that chance away from us. We need someone who will take us in and care for us. That person is Jesus. But mostly, I learned a lot about my relationship with God through this adoption. I came to know Abba Father up close and personal.

The Bible speaks on several occasions of adoption....

"Long before He laid down earth's foundations, He had us in mind, and had settled on us as the focus of His love, to be made whole and holy by His love. Long, long ago He decided to adopt us into His family through Jesus Christ. (What pleasure He took in planning this!) He wanted us to enter into the celebration of His lavish gift-giving by the hand of His beloved Son."
Ephesians 1:3-6 The Message

"But when the time arrived that was set by God the Father, God sent His Son, born among us of a woman, born under the conditions of the law so that He might redeem those of us who have been kidnapped by the law. Thus we have been set free to experience our rightful heritage. You can tell for sure that you are now fully adopted as His own children because God sent the Spirit of His Son into our lives crying out, "Papa! Father!" Doesn't that privilege of intimate conversation with God make it plain that you are not a slave, but a child? And if you are a child, you're also an heir, with complete access to the inheritance."
Galatians 4:4-8 The Message

Adoption is the heart of God's message. It is the heart of the Gospel.

As I really thought about this, I came to realize that adoption mirrors Christ's adoption of us in several ways as well.

1. Adoption changes our status and changes our name.

Before our boys were adopted, they had a different last name. Before they were adopted they were in a completely desolate situation. It was hopeless. They had no certain or guaranteed future of a family. They were broken and torn.

However, once they were adopted, it all changed. They took on our last name. They no longer were orphans, but now they were part of a forever family. Their status was changed to accepted.

And just like that, it is the same with us. Before we are saved and adopted into His family, we are of the world. But once we become part of His family, all that changes. We become His. We take on His name. Our status changes. Everything changes.

My children have the same "belonging" as I do with my father. Now, my mother gave birth to me. I was raised with my birth parents. Nothing I could ever do would change the fact that I'm their daughter. Even though I may make bad choices, those choices never once change the fact that I belong to them. I never quit being my father's daughter.

It's the same with my boys. Just because they're adopted doesn't change anything. They are Ron and Stacy Fulton's children. No matter what they do, no matter what issues they may have, nothing will ever change the fact that they belong to us. And they always will. Their choices or their issues don't define who they are. The bottom line is that they are identified as our children. Period.

It applies just as equal to our relationship with God.

2. Adoption makes us heirs of the Father.

When we adopted the boys and everything became legal, they then became a rightful heir to all that we have. They have access to anything we own. They don't have to ask to get to something to eat. They can go to the refrigerator and eat anytime they want. They don't have to ask to have a bed to sleep in. We provide that for them. They don't have to ask us to provide for their needs. It's a given. We clothe them. We feed them. We meet all their needs without them ever having to ask one time. It's just what we do as parents.

I can't help but think of how that is so true with God. He will always take care of us because He is our Father. We never have to worry about anything. He knows what we need and He will take care of it.

> "That is why I tell you not to worry about everyday
> life—whether you have enough food and drink, or
> enough clothes to wear. Isn't life more than food and
> your body more than clothing? Look at the birds. They
> don't plant or harvest or store food in barns, for your
> heavenly Father feeds them. And aren't you far more
> valuable to him than they are? Can all your worries add
> a single moment to your life? And why worry about
> your clothing? Look at the lilies of the field and how
> they grow. They don't work or make their clothing, yet
> Solomon in all his glory was not dressed as beautifully as
> they are. And if God cares so wonderfully for wildflowers
> that are here today and thrown into the fire tomorrow,
> he will certainly care for you. Why do you have so little
> faith? So don't worry about these things, saying, 'What
> will we eat? What will we drink? What will we wear?'
> These things dominate the thoughts of unbelievers,

but your heavenly Father already knows all your needs.
Seek the Kingdom of God above all else, and live
righteously, and He will give you everything you need."
Matthew 6:25-33

How comforting to think of it that way! It brings my heart
great peace in knowing how He will take care of me when I
think of it in terms of how I take care of my kids.

Just like my boys are now heirs to everything we own, so it is
with us and our Father. All that He has is ours. It belongs to us.

"And if you are a child, you're also an heir,
with complete access to the inheritance."
Galatians 4:8

I love the beauty of how God works. He uses things that
happen in our lives to reveal truths to us about His heart for us
and His character. I absolutely love it. I also love how He shows
us different things through what He is doing.

I mentioned in a previous chapter about how I was asking
all the "why" questions. You know, "Why can't we have kids?"
"Why us?" Just why, why, why. But God did something really
neat through this process. He began to show us that while we
were asking our whys, there were children who were doing
the same thing. Children who were asking, "Why can't we
have parents?"

They have why questions, too. Once we realized this, we
realized how small our minds were in this whole thing. We had
been so focused on our problem, that we didn't even realize
these children were basically doing the same thing. And it
broke our hearts. But, thankfully, God had a redemptive plan
in mind for us.

Being a photographer, I learn the most by pictures. They paint the story for me and I'm able to understand what it is I'm trying to learn. I've always been that way. I'm just grateful He teaches each of us according to how we're wired to learn.

So for our family? He painted a picture of redemption. He showed us a redemption for all of our questions. He painted a picture of His grace and mercy at work. He made it personal.

Chapter 8

GRACE

"He said, 'My grace is all you need. My power
works best in weakness'. So now I am glad
to boast about my weaknesses, so that the
power of Christ can work through me."
2 Corinthians 12:9

SINCE THE ADOPTION, LIFE has not been the same!
That's an obvious statement. People always ask me what it was
like to get three boys at the same time, all different ages and at
different stages of life. I always jokingly reply, "It's like getting
in a barrel and going off of Niagara Falls with both hands
raised. It's the ultimate adventure!" And an adventure it is.
Going from a quiet house with just a couple of dogs to having
a home filled with three young boys and all the "boy" things
you can imagine, well, it makes for quite the difference! There
has been tons of laughter and much joy. But one thing is for
sure; they have made my house a home.

When we got the boys, they were all involved in some sort of therapy. Some was speech therapy for stuttering, some was occupational therapy for learning to communicate, and then we were also meeting with a counselor for other various issues. So we have been involved in some type of therapy from the beginning.

Since the adoption, we have dealt with new issues. Of course we still had the boys in their speech therapies and such, but we eventually began seeing new issues develop. We had to start dealing with some attachment and emotional issues that seemed to have come on at early ages. Then there was just some behavioral things that required direct attention.

Over the course of time, I have learned that some of these issues are beyond me. They are beyond what a hug and a kiss can take care of and make well. They are requiring a different intervention altogether. I'll just be honest…it has gotten the best of me at times.

We have had to deal with some more extreme issues with the youngest. I always try to relate to what he's gone through in his life. I mean, at seven weeks old he was taken away from his mother and placed in foster care. I was the fifth mother he knew. I can't imagine what goes on inside of his little heart sometimes. The fears and all the things he probably doesn't even realize he's feeling, they all play a part in his actions. But as frustrating as things can be with him at times, one thing never changes and always remains the same…my love for that child is insane. I am head-over-heels-crazy about him. It doesn't matter what he has done, when he flashes that smile at me, nothing matters. Even if it has nothing to do with what he has done, but maybe I'm just having a bad day, when he comes and smiles at me and loves on me, my world is complete.

As I'm writing this book, we are coming off of one of the most intense times since the adoption. So intense, that it has put me on my face, and on my knees. It has caused me to go running to His presence to find help, strength and grace and wisdom.

This past year, things were just escalating a little more. We were having issues in school with our grades, we started noticing some uncontrollable tics in one of the boys, and we had some other things happening that just gave us much concern. All of this eventually led us to some doctor appointments last summer that, in return, gave me answers I didn't really want to hear.

Nothing was super disastrous, but enough to shake me up a little. In about a two month time period, we were diagnosed with Tourettes syndrome, ADHD and Aspergers. Again, nothing super disastrous, but a lot for a momma to take in all at once. And for this momma? It was a lot. A whole lot.

Now, let me back up for a moment and just state this obvious fact: I am the least qualified woman to be chosen as a parent. Especially for these particular kids. I'm undomesticated, I'm lazy, I'm selfish and I have a lot of baggage. Why God would choose me to parent these three boys I'll never know. I would never have picked me. There are seas of other women who are more qualified than me to do this job. Raising a child that is your own flesh and blood, who has no baggage is one thing. Raising a child that has a chance from the start and never experiences abuse and rejection and terrifying circumstances is altogether a different thing than what I was given. God, in all His wisdom, instead of giving me the ability to have a child naturally, chose to grant my desire to be a mom through a means of adoption. And not just any adoption, He chose three children who had lived through hell and experienced things in their short years that most of us will never experience in our entire lives. They came with baggage. They came with issues. Yet, for some reason, God picked me. Because of it, I have become so aware of His grace. I have fallen into the arms of His grace day after day after day because I am constantly making wrong choices. I mess up, I blow it so many times. I am constantly running back and forth to the mercy seat of Christ to seek forgiveness and wisdom.

This is so far out of my range. I'm not good at grace myself. My faith is not like that of most women. I'm not wise by any means. I'm inconsistent. I'm just not the most likely to succeed when it comes to something like this. But here I was. Here I am.

Grace is a beautiful thing. It covers our weaknesses. It covers our mistakes. It is bountiful and endless. It is full of love. And best of all – it is free. It's a gift we are all given day after day. Straight from the Father's heart to ours. Without it, I'd be a complete mess. And so would you.

God purposefully does things in our lives to show Himself strong. He provides opportunities that our flesh cannot handle, just so He can show us how strong He is. He allows "Goliaths" to come into our lives, those giants that seem to scream that they are bigger than anything, just so He can show us that He is bigger than our Goliaths. He allows us to come upon a Red Sea, with our enemy closing in and we think there is no escape, just so He can show His glory by parting the sea and providing a way of escape. He challenges our devotion and obedience by asking us to lay our most treasured possessions upon the altar, just so He can provide the sacrifice and show His faithfulness. He allows us to be carried upon a caravan that seems like a great detour from the path we think we should be on, just so He can refine us and develop us to be vessels that are ready to step into the destiny He has for our lives. He gives us opportunities to partner with Him, to allow His strength to become our own, so that we can see how great and mighty He truly is.

I have always questioned God about why He chose me. He sent me a divine interruption with infertility and then gave me these children. He knew what they would deal with and what issues they would have, yet He still chose me. Not because I was qualified. He chose me because in His grace, He knew that this had a divine purpose that was far beyond my natural abilities to bring about. It has a kingdom purpose.

God did not choose me to mother a newborn baby, born of my flesh. He did not choose me to mother a child who was normal by the world's standards. I did not get to experience the things that most mothers get to walk through and enjoy. I didn't have nine months of experiencing a child growing inside of me. I didn't get to experience the birthing process. None of what I have gone through has been normal according to a worldly viewpoint.

He provided a door to motherhood through a completely different means for me. One, that if given the option, I would probably have never chosen, but knowing what I do now, could not imagine my life any different. He didn't lead me on a journey that would satisfy my earthly and natural instincts. Instead, He led me on a journey to motherhood that was far beyond my wildest dreams or imaginations. He led me on a journey that would not only change the lives of three young boys, but ultimately would change mine as well. He led me to motherhood through the pathway of the Father's heart.

Knowing that nothing about my life is normal, I choose to remain hidden in the fact that His plans far exceed any I could dream. Yes, some days are hard. Some days I am tempted to run. Some days I question His plans. But it's only when I'm looking at my own limitations and not focusing on the fact that the One Who called me is faithful to complete what He's doing that I see potential failure. We have to remember that if He calls us to do something, He goes with us. His presence will always go before us, and continue to walk with us through the entire journey.

I know that I can't be the mother to these boys that I should based on my own strength. I have too much baggage, I have too many faults, and I am weak. But the wondrous thing about our Father is that He knows all of these things even before He chooses us. Before He set things in motion for me to become a mom, He knew all of my shortcomings. He knew all of my weaknesses. He chose me anyway. He chose me because He knew I couldn't do this on my own strength. It would only be by the working of His strength and power within me that I could carry out the task He has laid before me.

Fast forward to today. I'm almost at a loss for words at how God showed Himself to me today.

The last several years we have had a little more severe emotional and behavioral issue with one of the boys. So much so, that we suspect there is some behavioral disorders, with a possibility of bipolar disorder being present. I have fought and fought this in my head for a long time. I didn't want to be given that diagnosis. The reasons were selfish, really. I didn't want the stigma of having a child that was labeled as bipolar. I didn't want to have to deal with a child who was bipolar. It was all about me. I wasn't thinking about the one who this affected even greater…my son.

I have had a few breakdowns in recent days and weeks regarding this. It's just been more than I could bear emotionally at times. I just want my children to be normal, healthy and happy. You know, like everyone else's kids. I don't want them to have to go through life dealing with effects of their past. And honestly, I just wasn't ready to walk through it myself.

I was looking at the issue and the problem and focusing in on all the things surrounding it. I was failing to look beyond it all to see what may be awaiting me through another uncharted territory. I was choosing not to see that I had once again walked into another period of darkness, another stormy sea, another opportunity to find a hidden treasure.

So, today we had an appointment with a therapist at a local mental health institution. The name alone makes my skin crawl with feelings of uneasiness about what I'm about to encounter. Up until today I was just fearing the future of what was coming.

When I woke up today I spent some time talking to God about this whole thing. For so long I have asked Him to completely heal all of my children. I've asked Him to set them free from any attachments of their past. I've asked Him to erase what happened to them in their past. As we celebrated our seven year anniversary of our adoption last May, I truly believed He was going to do a mighty miraculous healing then. I was set on the fact of the number seven being significant of completion and having to do with jubilee, that I had set my heart on the fact that He would do something amazing through it all.

However, we are almost through the end of this eighth year now, and we are still fighting battles. We still face the same obstacles everyday. Weariness has set in. Until today.

When I woke up and began to pray today, my heart was different. I had a long conversation with God about it all. I proceeded to express my faith in His ability to heal. I knew that one touch from Him could completely heal my boys of anything they are going through. I knew He could speak one word and they would be set free. I fully believe He is able to do it.

But I also believe in His sovereignty. And in His sovereignty, He chooses to do things different than I might always choose. Just like I saw in how He brought our family together. I walked through infertility to find a pathway to His heart. That pathway eventually led me to my children. It was all in His sovereignty and His divine Kingdom purposes.

So today I declared His sovereignty over this situation. I placed my trust in His ability to carry me through, regardless of the outcome. I had to put all of this in His hands and at His feet. I had to turn my heart to be in complete submission to whatever He chose to do with this. Was it easy? No. I just did it in faith, with no feelings attached.

We got to the appointment and went in and got settled in the waiting room. The whole time I'm just thinking, "This isn't us. This isn't the way our family should have to live. We should be dealing with colds and viruses and little things. Not something like this." As soon as I could get the thoughts through my head I had to lay them back down. After all, the enemy knew my weak point in this and these were all just part of his tactic to draw my heart away from my heavenly Father.

The therapist made her way up front and came and got us. The walk back to her office made me a little nervous. I just didn't know what I was about to discover as we dove head first into this behavioral issue.

As we got into her office and sat down, she began asking me a series of questions. It was all to gather a clear history so they would know how to proceed. As I was talking with her and answering the questions, I noticed she had what appeared to be a small, raggedy little stuffed lion. The kind like you would get in a happy meal or something. It was nothing special and at first I just didn't think much of it. So I kept on with our conversation. A few more minutes into it, my eyes just happened to look up above her desk at the picture hanging on the wall. What was it? It was a large, framed print of nothing else, but a lion.

Now, I suppose I should stop here and do some explaining. I mentioned lions in a previous chapter, but I didn't tell you how much lions have played a part in so much of what God has done in my life through the years.

I am a BIG fan of Aslan and the *Chronicles of Narnia*. I can almost recite the movies I've seen them so many times. I love the picture he paints of Jesus and how He is the Lion of Judah. I love the different ways that He reveals His majesty and His ability to do the impossible by the roar He lets out. I love that I can't look at a lion picture and NOT see the eyes of the greatest Lion of all. He is King of all Kings and He rules above everything.

I was blessed to be able to go to Africa last August with our church. It was my first mission trip out of the country and it was life changing in so many ways. But on the trip, on our last day there, we had the opportunity to go on a Lion Walk. And it is just what it says; you literally walk with real, live, breathing lions. It was incredible.

I remember thinking that if one of these lions began speaking to me I would most certainly be raptured on the spot. The funny thing is, I went into it thinking I wouldn't be surprised if it DID start speaking to me! (guess I've watched Aslan a few times too many)

In the past few months with everything going on with the boys, there was a new song my friend had introduced me to called, "Always." This song has become the new song of my life for this particular season. It talks of how my God will always come through, and how I will not fear because His promises are true. It is just right on to the truths I am holding dear in my heart right now.

My best friend, Lori, is a lion chaser as well. She loves lions as much as I do. So for her birthday, which I might add, happens to be the exact same day as mine, I made her a canvas with one of the pictures of a lion I took in Africa and the words to this song. Unbeknownst to me, my business partner and dear friend, Shana, took my file and surprised me with the same thing. I have this picture hanging in our apartment right now. It serves as my daily reminder that He WILL come through. He WILL sound a victorious roar when all is said and done. He will not disappoint. He will fulfill His promises to me and our family.

Which brings me back to today. As soon as I looked up and saw the picture hanging above her desk, I immediately felt the Lord speak to me and say, "You may be walking into a fire, but you won't come out burned. There is a fourth man in your fire Who won't leave your side. You may be stepping into a den of lions, but they won't harm you because I will shut their mouths. And you will walk out unharmed. You have no need to fear, because I'm with you."

I was stunned. I was amazed. Then I was humbled. Humbled that the God of the universe, the God of all creation, took such great care and detail in speaking so directly to me today. He knew the significance of the lion in my life, and of all places for us to end up in this building, He chose to put us in with a therapist who loves lions. He made it personal today. He gave me yet another kairos moment in that room. And at that exact moment, I chose to keep walking right beside Him.

I have no idea what the days and weeks ahead are going to be like. I don't know how hard things will get. I don't know what we're going to encounter. All I know is this:

> "The LORD is my shepherd;
> I have all that I need.
> He lets me rest in green meadows;
> He leads me beside peaceful streams.
> He renews my strength.
> He guides me along right paths,
> bringing honor to His name.
> Even when I walk
> through the darkest valley,
> I will not be afraid,
> for You are close beside me.
> Your rod and your staff
> protect and comfort me.
> You prepare a feast for me
> in the presence of my enemies.
> You honor me by anointing my head with oil.
> My cup overflows with blessings.
> Surely Your goodness and unfailing love will pursue me
> all the days of my life,
> and I will live in the house of the LORD forever."
> Psalms 23

This is all I could recite today. These words are just overflowing from my heart. The more I have read them, the more that I see they have guided me through this entire journey from the start.

He has been the good Shepherd to me all along. In the abundant and peaceful times He has been there. He was leading me from the beginning. He leads me along the right paths that bring honor to HIS name. Even when I encounter darkness and I am walking through the darkest valley, I have no reason to fear or be afraid. He is always close to me. He is always beside me. His authority protects me and His arms comfort me no matter what place I find myself in at the time. His unfailing love will always pursue me. And I will live and reign with Him forever.

Wow. Just wow. This is one of those moments when I need to just sit and sigh because there really aren't any words that are adequate to describe what's going on in my heart right now. All I can do is bask in the greatness of Who He is and what He's done for me. All I can do is throw myself onto the wings of faith and trust in what He's going to do in me and through me during this process.

I don't have it all together by any means. I don't have all the answers to what's going on in our lives. I've encountered enough to know that hard days will come. My faith will be tested and my enemy will be relentless in his attempts to draw my heart and my affections away from my Father. He will try to muster up lies and twist the truth. But the one thing he doesn't have this time is a naïve little girl who has no clue who she is in Christ. On the contrary, this time he's dealing with a woman who knows her place in the kingdom. She knows who her Father is, and she understands that nothing can separate her from His great love. Nothing. She understands that in His great love for her, sometimes things happen she may not be able to comprehend at the time, but in the end, she knows that her times and her life are in HIS hands. She has seen His ability to carry her through the roughest moments, and He remains faithful to the end.

So yeah, the enemy will bring it, I'm sure. But this time I'm prepared for battle.

One thing that I love about how God speaks is that it never fails He will confirm His word. Last year, for the first time ever, I read the through the entire bible in a year. I have the One Year Bible, New Living Translation, and it was the greatest feeling to complete it last year and then start all over again January 1st.

The cool thing I have discovered while doing this is that it seems everyday the selected readings have something to do with what's going on in my life. One day it might be something I read in the Old Testament. The next day it may be the New Testament that does it. Or it could be one of the Psalms or Proverbs for the day. And then somedays it could just be some of all of it! But regardless, He speaks through His word.

Today was no different. The Old Testament reading is in Genesis right now and guess what story we are on? Joseph. Yep, there's Joseph again. At the exact time I'm writing this book. It's been great walking back through his story.

The Psalms for today is what is so perfect though. The passage for today is Psalm 18:16-36. It immediately grabbed my attention.

"He reached down from heaven and rescued me; He
drew me out of deep waters. He delivered me from my
powerful enemies, from those who hated me and were
too strong for me. They attacked me at a moment when
I was weakest, but the Lord upheld me. He led me to a
place of safety; He rescued me because He delights in me."
Psalm 18:16-19

"Lord, You have brought light to my life;
my God, You light up my darkness.
In Your strength I can crush an army;
with my God I can scale any wall.
As for God, His way is perfect. All the
Lord's promises prove true. He is a shield
for all who look to Him for protection.
For Who is God except the Lord? Who
but our God is a solid rock?
God arms me with strength; He has made my
way safe. He makes me as surefooted as a deer,
leading me safely along the mountain heights.
He prepares me for battle; He strengthens
me to draw a bow of bronze. You have
given me a shield of Your salvation.
Your right hand supports me; Your
gentleness has made me great.
You have made a wide path for my feet
to keep them from slipping."
Psalm 18:28-36

Wow, right off the bat He is confirming what He spoke
to me yesterday in that doctor visit. Right off the bat He is
repeating everything He said as I was writing yesterday. And
yet again, He shows me that He does not call me to do these

things alone. He does not ask me to join Him on this journey to walk alone.

Instead, He asks me to walk behind Him, covered in Him, as I travel down darkened roads and through uncertain times. He is a shield for me, yes, but He is also my guide, leading me through darkness.

THE TREASURES

The Treasures

"We are pressed on every side by troubles, but
we are not crushed. We are perplexed, but not
driven to despair. We are hunted down, but never
abandoned by God. We get knocked down, but we
are not destroyed. Through suffering, our bodies
continue to share in the death of Jesus so that the
life of Jesus may also be seen in our bodies."

"That is why we never give up. Though our bodies are
dying, our spirits are being renewed every day. For our
present troubles are small and won't last very long. Yet
they produce for us a glory that vastly outweighs them
and will last forever! So we don't look at the troubles
we can see now; rather, we fix our gaze on things that
cannot be seen. For the things we see now will soon be
gone, but the things we cannot see will last forever."
2 Corinthians 4:8-10, 16-18

So, after all the years of walking through infertility, all the
ups and downs and tragedies and triumphs, what do I walk

away with? I want to spend this last section telling you how I've learned to apply all the things I've come to know and understand through the journey, and for all the things still yet to come. The great thing about hearing someone else tell their story is sometimes maybe we can learn from their mistakes so we don't have to find ourselves making the same ones.

I don't have this figured out completely by any means. I'm far from it. All I have is the basis of the things I have found traveling my own paths down darkened roads and uncharted waters. My hope is that through what I have come to understand through my journey, you will be able to use in navigating your own.

I titled this section what I did because there truly are power and treasures to be found in our brokenness. There are some valuable lessons we can learn while walking through dark valleys, and while on this journey, there are some pearls of great price and some beautiful truths we can find buried in the heart of God for our lives.

I love how those verses above just ooze hope within them. I love how we find things "unseen" in our valleys. In our darkest moments really. It's those treasures hidden in darkness we've talked about all along. Those things that we can only find in the dark times of our lives. It's in the darkest times of our lives that we find out what faith in Him truly is. It's in dark times that we find out how good He is, even when life doesn't always agree. It's in dark times that we learn the value of pressing through, seeking His face and finding His heart. For THAT, my friend, is the greatest treasure of all. When we find His heart through the dark valleys, we have found our pearl of great price. And sometimes those great pearls come at the expense of our comforts. They come when we are the weakest. But they DO come—when we are seeking Him through it.

Verses 8-10 give me even greater hope. Battles may get intense. They always do. There's always blood shed in war. There are casualties. There are injuries and wounds inflicted from enemy fire. There are times when the soldiers grow weak and tired and weary. There are times when daylight never shines because the enemy fire is intense and keeps the sun hidden by all the artillery being unleashed, by all the smoke from the fire. BUT, here's where we find hope: we may be pressed in on every side by enemy fire—but we aren't crushed. We may be filled with uncertainty and facing difficulties in our lives by what we are going through—but it does not have to drive us to despair. We may be hunted down day and night by our enemy—but we are NEVER abandoned by our great and mighty Warrior...Father God. We may get knocked down—A LOT—but it does not destroy us. We get back up. Why? Because greater is He Who lives in us, than our enemy who lives in the world.

Bottom line...HE is stronger. He is able. And He fights for us. He is our great Defender.

I write all of this tonight with a heart that is screaming, "Fill me with THIS hope in the midst of battle!" To stand on the battleground and lean on, and rely on the fact that never once will He ever leave us in the battle. He gives us the weapons to use to fight our enemy, and then He gives us the strength and wisdom to fight according to His ways, not ours.

Chapter 9

THE HEART OF THE FATHER

*Times of brokenness provide an opportunity
to discover Who God is.*

WHEN MY HEART WAS broken with the news I'd never have a child, it sent me on a journey. At the time it was a journey I wasn't prepared or expecting to embark upon, but I was forced to pack up my bags from the place I was spiritually and hit the road whether I wanted to or not. God knew that staying in the same place I was would only allow my heart to become stagnant and stale. And in His great love for me, He knew my heart longed for more deep down. He knew I was made for more.

Pain has a way of opening our hearts to search for God whether we realize it or not. Some people turn to other things when they're hurting, but ultimately, what their hearts are truly longing so desperately to find is one thing…God.

So He begins to draw us to Himself. He uses the circumstances of our lives to draw us to His heart.

At first, we have no idea that He is drawing us. As a matter of fact, at first sight, it may look as though He has abandoned us. Things happen in our lives and the more intense and difficult, we seem to start pointing fingers at God and asking Him why these things are happening in the first place. From the outside, it looks as if He has turned His back on us, letting us fight for ourselves. It sometimes appears that our present circumstances are so great, that a loving God would have prevented them from happening in the first place.

But let me stop here and interject something. Bad things do happen in this world. Friends and loved ones die. Spouses cheat and leave us. Employers decide to terminate positions. The doctors give us a grim diagnosis. Children get abused. Tragedies strike. Our hearts get broken and our dreams DO get shattered.

While I can't explain why these things always happen, one thing I know for sure. We live in a world that is evil. This world has the prince of darkness at work attempting to destroy all hope and completely annihilate our relationship with God. He is an enemy out to destroy us.

"The thief comes only in order to steal, kill and destroy..."
John 10:10 AMP

His sole purpose is to destroy us -- to steal our dreams, to kill our faith and to destroy our destinies. He is bent on our destruction.

On top of that truth, people have choices. They have free wills. Sometimes we make good choices, sometimes we make bad ones. But the beauty in Christ's redemption is our free will because it ultimately provides a means for His grace to be so evident in our lives.

So, having said all of that, we'll settle on the fact that bad things just happen.

Circumstances out of our control invade our lives and force us to make the journey into darkness. Divine detours lead us to places we would never have chosen to travel, but they are places full of abundance in Him. They are places filled with treasures beyond our wildest dreams.

Now, all that is great to know, but the real question lies in this:

How do we find God in the midst of all this?

We have to begin seeking. It's that simple. Is it easy? No. But it is necessary if we are to find Him.

"You will seek Me and you will find Me
when you seek Me with all of your heart. I
will be found by you, declares the Lord."
Jeremiah 29:13-14

He draws us and begins wooing us through our circumstances. It's our part to start seeking Him through it. We must begin to seek Him above our circumstances. He must become bigger than what we are facing. And it's not easy to do. You literally have to search for Him like you would a buried treasure that you know if you find it, you will be set for life. Finding Him is THAT valuable.

We may not always understand His ways, or why He allows things to happen, but something happens in us when we set our questions like that aside and begin to focus our hearts on His.

When we begin to look at things through His perspective, it changes ours. I will tell you from first hand experience, when you choose Him above what you're longing for, or what you're praying for, you WILL come to know Him through it.

It wasn't until I laid aside my desire for a child and chose to seek Him instead that my life truly changed. I threw myself into His word; I spent time on my face in prayer asking Him to fill me with His heart, His desires, and His ways. I wanted the things of Him to occupy all the places within me. He had to come and mend to my broken heart. And as I laid myself at His feet and asked Him to pour Himself over me, He did just that. He healed my broken heart. He filled all the cracks with grace. He mended all areas that were damaged. All by His sweet presence as it permeated every part of me as I surrendered to Him.

May I just say that it's no different for you. No matter what situation you are facing, the only place to find rest and healing is at His feet, in His presence and through His Word. As you begin to bring all the broken pieces of your life and place them before Him, He takes them and turns your ashes into something beautiful.

It's through this process that we begin to uncover some vital truths about the nature of God.

1. He is unalterably good.
2. He is faithful.
3. He longs to bless us.

The battle we begin to face through this process, however, is to believe that God can be trusted, even when bad things happen. It's through the seeking of His heart and discovering Who He is that we come to know that He IS good.

You see, we must be able to call God good, even if we suffer. Not because of any other reason than this—HE IS! When things are going great and we are living in the land of abundance in our lives, do we have a problem thinking that He is good? Do we believe He is faithful? Yes. So when times turn and we enter times of brokenness and despair, why do we feel differently? It's because we haven't truly come to know these truths.

Nothing changes with God. He is the same yesterday, today and forever. So if He was good to you yesterday, He is still good today. If He is good to you today, He will still be good tomorrow. Nothing changes on His end. Nothing alters His character. Our perspective is what changes. When we are forced to look through life with shattered glasses, it seeks to alter our perception of Him and His nature. But once we come to truly know Him, then we know without a doubt that He is good regardless of where I find myself in life. Regardless of the situation, no matter how good or bad, He is still the same.

What does the bible say about the goodness of God?

All throughout the book of Psalms we see the goodness of God displayed. But these particular passages speak so clearly of it.

"Great is the Lord and most worthy of
praise. His greatness no one can fathom."
Psalm 145:3

"The Lord is gracious and compassionate; slow
to anger and rich in love. The Lord is good to
all; He has compassion on all He has made."
Psalm 145:8

"The Lord is near to all who call on Him,
to all who call on Him in truth."
Psalm 145:18

And here again, we see that His intentions are never to harm us…

"For I know the plans I have for you, declares
the Lord; plans to prosper you and not to harm
you; plans to give you a future and a hope."
Jeremiah 29:11

I won't say that events in our lives don't push us to a breaking point at times, but our struggle to believe that God is good does not change the unalterable truth that He is GOOD. His Word is our ultimate plumb line to measure our thoughts against the realities of Who He really is.

God is pursuing you. He is pursuing me. He is pursuing all of us. He pursues us not for His own pleasure. But rather, He pursues us so that we can find a soul satisfying intimacy with Him. He is looking for someone who will just believe. He pursues the broken and contrite so He can lead them to a path of discovering Him through their brokenness. And in His pursuit, He is looking for someone who will respond.

Will you respond? Will you lay down your questions and your false beliefs, and allow Him to take the ashes and turn them into something beautiful? Will you answer His call to come away and find Him through your journey?

It's where the real journey begins and the ordinary, stagnant, and mundane life you once knew ends.

My son has been reading a story about Hurricane Andrew for his reading class at school. It has been talking about how strong the hurricane was, how much destruction it brought. It talks about the strong gale force winds and how they ripped through power lines and shattered windows. The winds were so strong that they bent trees completely over. That's some strong and fierce wind right there. THAT, my friend, is a storm of epic proportions.

As I'm writing this chapter tonight, our area is under a severe storm watch. I'm thinking of the power of these types of storms. The way a storm can bring so much destruction and damage. How a storm can cause panic, fear, uncertainty and chaos. How scary it is when tornado sirens start going off to warn of impending danger. Then I started thinking about some dear friends who are facing some storms like that right now. In the last few months, I have friends who have been slammed by destructive winds, and tornadic level storms, and by floods of torrential rain in their families. It has done a lot to them emotionally and spiritually like kind of what Hurricane Andrew did in the physical realm. Kind of like what these storms approaching our area are threatening to do. It has caused fear. It has caused chaos and uncertainty. It has caused some pain. Damage has been done. But something strikes me about these types of storms in our lives. Something that, as a Christ follower, we get a rare opportunity to experience...if we choose to do so.

I've always loved the story about the disciples and being in the boat and the big storm comes. Matthew 14 gives us the story of how Jesus had sent the disciples on their way and how a huge storm with heavy winds and strong waves had come upon them. What we overlook a lot of times is that it said Jesus made His disciples get in the boat and cross to the other side. He led them into the storm.

Notice when He led them into the storm though—it was right after they had seen a miracle. They had been there with the 5,000 men, when there were only five loaves and two fish. They watched Him bless it and then hand it to them to go and feed the whole group. They learned a new truth about Him and His character that day. They learned He was more than what they had seen prior to this.

So He puts them in the boat and sends them across the sea to the other side. It tells us that when it was "evening" or "dark", a great storm came upon the waters and the boat was being tossed about by strong winds and waves. They had just been following Jesus, doing as He said, and from out of nowhere, they find themselves being tossed about in a fierce storm.

But something happens in the middle of the storm. It says "the disciples saw Him". In the middle of the storm they SAW Him. When Peter realizes it is Jesus, he tells Him to call him to come and walk to Him. It was here that my heart is always gripped by this story. It was here that Jesus tells Peter, "Come to Me." Now I'm sure at first Peter had to be like, "Huh? Really?" I would've been! But Peter does the impossible and gets out of the boat. He gets out of the safety net. He steps into uncharted territory. He walks into uncertainty. He goes towards Jesus.

Okay so think with me for a minute about this. Jesus calls Peter to come to Him. Jesus is in the very middle of this chaotic storm. Winds are howling. Rain is pouring. Waves are surging all around. The boat is being tossed about like a toy in the middle of it all. Yet there He stands. In the middle of this crazy storm...He stands. And He calls Peter to come to Him. He is telling Peter to leave the safety of the boat, to do something he's never done before, and to walk on a faith he's never seen. Walk on the water? Really? In the middle of a raging storm? Leave the safety of the boat and step into raging seas? Yes. Absolutely. And that's what He does for us as well. That's what He's doing for my friends who've recently been thrust into the middle of all the madness.

To think, when a tornado is upon you and human nature says to run, take shelter, take cover, keep safe, HE says, "Come to Me. Through the storm, come to Me." Who does something like that? Who asks you to step out into fierce winds, dangerous conditions...who asks you to run into the middle of the storm instead of taking shelter from the storm? He does. He does it because He knows that an encounter like this will change your life. It will change your faith. It will change everything. He knows that when you step into the middle of the darkest night, when you go running into the eye of a hurricane or the middle of tornadic activity in your life—He knows that what you find when you get there will be worth the struggle to get out of the boat. It will be worth the storm that started in the first place. It will be worth it all. And it will be worth it because there is a treasure waiting for you in the middle of this craziness that you could've never found had you not gotten out of the boat.

Crazy? Yeah, probably. But the encounter you have with the One Who bids you to come? Life altering. Worth it? Absolutely. Every part of it. You see, it's not easy to step out of the safety, or at least what you think is safe. And that "safety" is different for everyone. But He knows if you will trust Him, take the step, leap off the edge, you're going to learn to soar. You're going to learn to fly. You're going to learn something of Him that had you stayed in the boat, you'd never see.

It's through the storms that we learn Who He is. We learn His nature. We learn characteristics of Him. We come to know Him.

I love the ending to the story of the disciples and this storm. It says in verse 33, "They knelt and worshiped Him, saying, Truly You are the Son of God!" They discovered Who He was through the storm. And you and I will as well.

So as I'm sitting here watching the storms roll in tonight, I'm reminding myself of all these truths. I'm reminding myself that no matter the severity of the storm, I am not alone. I am not out from under His ever loving and ever seeing eye. His eyes are always on me. And though the storms may rage, my heart holds fast to His promises to never leave me nor forsake me.

Finding and discovering the heart of God in our lives does not mean that we are building our houses in a land without storms. Rather, it means that we are building our houses upon a rock and a foundational truth that no storm can destroy.

Grab hold of what you discover in the middle of the storm. It will become your anchor in the next storm you face.

Chapter 10

THE HEART OF WORSHIP

**Times of brokenness prepare a
stage for abandoned worship.**

WHEN LIFE IS HARD, it's even harder to sing. It's difficult to raise our hands in praise when we have nothing to be praising about. We get overwhelmed with the devastation that surrounds our lives at times, and trying to muster up any words of worship seems almost impossible.

When we are walking through the fire and in hard times, any form of worship is work. I mean let's just be honest and call it what it is. It is hard to worship when life is going wrong. It's much easier to focus on the negative. It's easier to complain and give up. It's easier to quit than it is to worship.

But what we don't realize is that worship is the fuel that keeps our lives going. When we discover how to worship in the midst of despair, it redefines us, it transforms us and it fills us with the ability to keep going, despite our circumstances.

I spoke a lot of how I learned to dance in the darkness of my life, how I learned how to dance on all the graves of what had died. It didn't come easy. I had to make the effort. I had to do something. I had to let go of all my heart held dear. I had to let Him have it before I could freely worship.

I did what all of us have to do at some point in our journeys. I opened my alabaster box and poured it at His feet.

I shared this passage earlier, but it is the passage that changed how I worshipped through my darkness.

"Sing, oh barren woman, who has never
had a baby. Fill the air with song, you
who've never experienced childbirth!
Isaiah 54:1a The Message

That verse is not just speaking to a woman unable to have a child. That verse speaks to all of us. It bids all of us to sing in the midst of adversity. When hope is silent, we sing. When joy is absent, we sing. When life is in turmoil, we sing. When we have nothing in us, when we are in a barren land, we give to Him our song of praise.

A story that paints a beautiful picture of worship amidst barrenness is found in Mark 12. It is the story of the widow who gave all she had. The crowds had gathered and were casting their money into the treasury. It says many "rich" people were there throwing in large sums. But then it hits a big point:

"And a widow who was poverty stricken came and
put in two copper mites, the smallest of coins, which
together made half a cent. And He called His disciples
to Him and said to them, 'Truly and surely I tell

you, this widow, who is poverty stricken, has put
in more than all those contributing to the treasury.
For they all threw in out of their abundance; but
she, out of her deep poverty, has put in everything
that she had, even all she had on which to live."
Mark 12:42-44

The rich people here represent those walking in abundance. Times are good. They are able to give out of their abundance. Their worship costs them nothing really.

But here comes the widow, who has nothing. She is barren. She is walking through a time where she has nothing to give. Yet, she gives all she had. When life had her at a place of nothing, when her crops were bare, when her land was barren and empty, she gave all she had of herself and cast it at His feet.

Jesus saw it as precious. He saw it as more valuable than what those who were giving out of abundance had offered up. Not that what they gave wasn't worth anything, but He saw that giving out of your abundance is easy because it costs you nothing. When you give out of your barrenness, when you give out of your brokenness, it costs you everything. And THAT is a gift that touches our Father's heart.

So those times of brokenness when you have nothing left to give are a perfect opportunity to offer up a sacrifice, to give to Him out of your nothingness, and to touch His heart because of it.

I heard a new song (I know, it's hard to believe I'm talking about a song...again). It's called "Letting Go" by Darlene Zschech. All I can say is WOW. This song has just brought me back to that altar I built in my life many years ago. It was the altar where I laid down my dream to have a child. It was the altar where I let go of that dream I held closest to my heart. It was my most treasured possession in my alabaster box. But it was at this altar that I poured out that perfume. I poured it out at His feet and let it go. I took my hands off of it and let go of what I thought I controlled. I let go of the dream. And in it's place? I exchanged that dream for something even more beautiful. I found Him. I found His heart. I found His dreams.

Today I'm thinking about all these things...dreams, alabaster boxes, all the stuff that is nearest and dearest to our hearts, all the stuff that makes our hearts beat just a little faster when we think of them because they mean so much to us. I'm thinking of all the times I've had to build an altar to let one of them go. Now that doesn't always necessarily mean He's taking it away from me. It just means what it says, "I LET IT GO." I put it on the altar and left it with Him. I took my hands off of it, so He could put His hands on it. My hands on all the things I love most, my hands on all my dreams...it doesn't amount to much. But, HIS hands on all these things... have mercy.

It's hard to let go. It's hard to give up control that, in reality, we never had in the first place, but in our minds we think we did. It's hard to give up our dime store pearls that we think are so valuable. But if we could only realize the truth that He has the real deal in His hands He's waiting to give us in their place. He never asks us to give up something that He doesn't have something far better to replace it with. Now, that could be He replaces it with His peace, His comfort...I don't know. He knows what we need. And this one thing I have learned to be so very true....we can trust His heart for us. We can trust His promises. We can trust His Word.

Dying is never easy. Watching something die can be pure torture. Watching something we have had our hearts set on for so long, only to see that dream get shattered into a million tiny pieces will break our hearts into a million pieces. Could I offer another way to look at it though? What if it's through these times that we could actually see God better? If we opened our eyes to it anyway.

Being able to worship amidst difficult times is a gift. It's a gift we're given after we've seen the face of God in the midst of our storm. It's a gift we're given after we encounter Him face to face in the heart of our battle. You see, once you see Him in the middle of your storm, once you encounter Him beside you on the battlefield, once you come to KNOW Him, then THAT itself is the gift. Worship comes out of the revelation of that gift.

That's how it was for me. After I found Him and discovered His heart for me, I was so full of thankfulness and gratitude that I had no other desire but to dance. Once I had buried all my dreams at His feet, shoveled the last bit of dirt up on top of them and said goodbye, then I danced over them in His presence. It was opening up my alabaster box, taking out my most prized possession and pouring it at His feet.

I had seen His worth through my pain. I had been able to declare that He was still worthy of all of my praise no matter what my life looked like at the moment.

I know someone else who saw His worth. Mary saw His worth. She saw everything in Him that her heart desired. And so she gave all she had in response to it. The world looked at her and thought she was crazy. Even the disciples thought she was crazy. But Mary didn't care. She knew that He had given her everything, and so nothing she had was valuable enough to keep anymore.

> "Meanwhile, Jesus was in Bethany at the home of
> Simon, a man who had previously had leprosy. While
> he was eating, a woman came in with a beautiful
> alabaster jar of expensive perfume and poured it over his
> head. The disciples were indignant when they saw this.
> "What a waste!", they said. "It could have been sold
> for a high price and the money given to the poor." But
> Jesus, aware of this, replied, "Why criticize this woman
> for doing such a good thing to Me? You will always
> have the poor among you, but you will not always have
> Me. She has poured this perfume on Me to prepare
> My body for burial. I tell you the truth, wherever the
> Good News is preached throughout the world, this
> woman's deed will be remembered and discussed."
> Matthew 26:6-13

The world will do the same to you and I when they see us in extravagant worship during difficult times. When the world sees you pouring your life at the feet of Jesus when all of your circumstances tell you to be angry or depressed or something else, they don't understand. They won't understand until they see His value. No one will.

It doesn't make sense to walk in peace when your life is tossed about by gale force winds of tragedy. It doesn't make sense to carry a smile on your face when your life has given you no reason to smile. The only thing that makes sense is Him. He is the common denominator in it. He is the One Who gives us peace that passes our understanding. He is the One Who promises us that joy will come in the morning. As a matter of fact, I like to say that He will give us joy in the 'mourning.' Because that's what He does.

And so in response to our understanding of Who He is, and how worthy He is of all we have, we dance. We sing. We offer praises. We pour out our lives at His feet. It doesn't matter if we can see the outcome to our situations. We don't need to know what the future will hold. We only need to know the One Who holds our future in His hands.

Difficult situations can turn your life upside down. Being led into a raging storm can shake your faith. It can cause you to feel abandoned and left alone. But if we can look beyond our circumstances, if we can wipe the rain from our face and look out into the middle of the storm, we see Jesus coming into the middle of our raging seas. Once we catch a glimpse of Him, it changes everything. And it inspires songs of praise.

> "The whole earth is filled with awe at Your
> wonders; where morning dawns, where
> evening fades, You inspire songs of praise."
> Psalm 65:8

If you would've asked me a few months ago if I believed that Jesus heals, I would've said yes. With complete assurance in my heart, it would've been yes. Not because I've had it happen to me personally, but because His word assures me it is possible. So I would've said yes based on that fact alone. Now, fast forward to today. If you ask me that same question, I will wholeheartedly declare a resounding YES, because not only does His word assure me of it, but I have now seen His word in action in my life personally. I have been a recipient of His touch. And let me just tell you, its one thing to know it based off of reading His word and hearing stories from other people. It's a completely different thing to know it based off a personal experience of it.

Back in November of last year I encountered another raging storm in my life. I had been battling an extremely intense illness for several weeks. To make a long story short, I'll just give you the cliff notes. I was sent to a top notch facility in Birmingham on a Wednesday for what was thought to be a hepatic liver abscess. Doctors found a lesion on my liver that instigated several imaging scans and with my symptoms continuing to worsen by the day, they felt a transfer to a hospital where people experienced in infectious disease could do a liver biopsy and treat me would be the best possible solution. No one in our area was experienced with it, and so off we went.

When we left that day, I have to admit, I was scared. We were faced with the uncertainty of what was going on, with an uncertainty of what was going to happen. My eyes were clouded by the fog of my current circumstances. I knew God was with me, but still my heart began to fear. However, I belong to a faithful God, and He knew what my heart needed, exactly when it needed it. And so after getting the news that I was being transferred and admitted, I began sending out messages to everyone I knew. My church met with us and prayed over me before we left. Everyone I know began praying and calling on other people to pray. Word spread quickly and before I knew it, I was surrounded by an army of believers, locked arm in arm, crying out to God on my behalf.

I don't know about you, but I've never walked through anything like this that required such faith and prayer. Infertility was one thing, but a serious illness that could ultimately take my life was another. Up until this point in my life, I had never battled serious physical illness, so I really didn't know how to walk in this. But as people began to pray, things began to change. My heart was encouraged and strengthened. And before we left for Birmingham, my husband and I both agreed, we weren't going to Birmingham for my healing, we were going to bring glory to God. We were going to make much of Jesus through this. If I was healed in the process, great. If I wasn't, that was ok too. We knew God was in this and we trusted Him to lead us through. He didn't leave my side the entire time.

There were moments as I lay in the hospital bed that as I closed my eyes, I could sense Him standing at the foot of my bed, just smiling over me. Like any good dad would do for his kid, here stood my Dad, standing at the foot of my bed, smiling over me, giving me the constant assurance that He would never leave my side. And He never did. His presence filled my room every moment I was there. My phone would constantly be going off with texts and messages coming through of people telling me they were praying and just encouraging me in my faith. When I say it was an army, I'm not kidding. I saw the army suit up and go to war on my behalf. THAT is humbling.

A few days prior to this, I saw a movie about war. It was about Sparta and a group of soldiers who were defending Sparta. They were fierce soldiers, who marched into battle with no fear, but always arm to arm in battle. It was no coincidence I saw this movie when I did. Because little did I know I was about to experience an army of believers suit up on my behalf and push back the enemy who was coming against me. And that is exactly what happened. People I knew, people I didn't know, all on their knees, crying out to God, swords drawn, shields raised, running onto the battlefield for ME. I'm still in complete amazement by it.

Well, I'm happy to say, it was a battle well fought. I was admitted on Wednesday and Thursday late afternoon my doctors came into the hospital room and told me this: "You came in with all the signs and symptoms of a hepatic liver abscess. Yet now your blood work shows nothing abnormal. Our radiologists have looked at all your scans and imaging, and they believe this spot on your liver to be just a benign hemangioma. Your liver is normal and healthy." And shortly after I was released from the hospital.

In the course of my stay I began to continuously improve. The doctors had done nothing. I had received no medicines. Nothing. And yet I was improving. The pain was subsiding; I was coming back to life. My symptoms began disappearing. Thursday morning a friend of mine had sent me a post on facebook that said this...

> *"From my devotion this morning..." He generally waits to send His help until the time of our greatest need, so that His hand will be plainly seen in our deliverance. He chooses this method so we will not trust anything that we may see or feel, as we are so prone to do, but will place our trust solely on His Word."*

The doctors had even came into my room and told me they weren't doing anything for me. Boy were they right! THEY weren't doing anything. It was completely the hand of my God at work, in response to the prayers being offered on my behalf. My army that had suited up to go into battle for me, they were pushing back the enemy with the power of God at work through them.

This was a place I had never been. I've had to trust God before on things, but never like this. I knew He would be with me. I just wanted to glorify Him through it however I could. And I wanted the whole thing to make much of His Name regardless of the outcome. And assuredly, it has indeed.

Wednesday morning I wasn't sure what would happen with me I was so sick. I had lost about eight pounds in less than a week. I was sick. Really sick. And yet by Thursday night I was on my way home because God had touched my life and made me whole.

My faith was tested for sure. I had to step out when I didn't see anything to step onto and just trust His hand to guide me through this. I found a lot of things during this dark moment. Several treasures found hidden in these darkest moments that I would not otherwise have found. Kind of like Peter. You have to step out of the boat and into the stormy waves to learn that you can, in fact, walk on the waves of adversity when you fix your eyes on the One Who can stand in the midst of the chaos and summons you to come and experience Him like never before. But as long as you stay in the boat, you'll never learn that miracles await those who walk by faith. Is it scary? Yes, when you only look around and see the chaos and stormy waves on all sides. But, when we step out, and our gaze becomes fixated on Him, the waves of adversity disappear, you don't care where your next step will be because you're walking on the certainty of the One Who has reached for you. You walk with the assurance that He will be the ground beneath your feet.

I also found healing through this dark moment. It is indeed a treasure. I would not know healing if I didn't walk through a time of needing to be healed. I would not know Jesus as my Healer any other way. But now, I can sing with a confident assurance, "I believe You're my healer, I believe You are all I need..." Before all of this, I sang that song based on head knowledge really. I believed that He healed. But now? Now I will sing that song with it permanently etched into my heart because now I KNOW Him as a Healer. And I'd go through months of being sick to find it out all over again.

The bottom line in all of this craziness? It's ALL worth it friends. Every trial we go through. Every dark night we encounter. They're all worth it when we find Him in the midst of it. Dark times can be scary, but you can always rest assured of one certain thing....morning WILL come. The sun WILL rise. ALWAYS.

I posted Psalm 65:8 at the beginning of this story. It just so happens that my room number in the hospital was 658. So I looked it up in the bible and found this verse. It was quite appropriate. So appropriate, in fact, that I'll write it here again for you....

> "The whole earth is filled with awe at Your
> wonders; where morning dawns, where
> evening fades, You inspire songs of praise."
> Psalm 65:8

He is a mighty God. He is a Healer. His name is Jesus. He has the power to do the impossible my friend. Throughout this journey, He has indeed inspired many songs of praise. His hand has moved on my behalf, and because of it, I had a facebook page that was lit up with nothing but songs of praise to my Jesus. Post after post after post, all declaring the greatness of my God. So yeah, this whole sickness...was it worth it? Absolutely. Because my God was glorified through it and at the end of the day, His great Name has inspired many, many songs of praise.

Now, I tell you that story to tell you this, I didn't just walk on the waves to go out and meet Him through that sickness. I danced on the waves as I gave Him praise through it all. I learned from my journey with infertility that He is good no matter what my circumstances look like. I had learned that I could trust Him and that He was always near. I had learned to dance regardless of what life looked like. So that's what I did that day on the way to Birmingham. We filled our car with sounds of praise. We decided beforehand to honor God with our lives, no matter the outcome we would see. I had no idea if I would be healed, if I would get worse, or if I might could possibly have died. None of that mattered when I latched onto the truths I already knew about Him.

I had seen Him in my life before. So when He called to me in the middle of the storm, I could dance my way to Him. I knew His heart. And I knew if He was calling me, He had a purpose awaiting me that was bigger than I could see.

I believe when we began declaring praises that day in the car He began to respond. Now, He doesn't always respond the same way. But on that day, He responded to my worship with healing in His hands. You see I was stretching out my hands giving Him what was before me. I was laying my life down at His feet. He responded by giving life back to me.

Abandoned worship will never return void. It may not bring with it the answer to your prayers, but it is sure to bring one thing, and that thing is the only necessary thing anyway. Your worship will bring you Jesus.

"They who sow in tears shall reap in joy and singing.
He who goes forth bearing seed and weeping
[at needing his precious supply of grain for sowing]
shall doubtless come again with rejoicing,
bringing his sheaves with him."
Psalm 126:5-6 AMP

Chapter 11

THE HEART OF MINISTRY

Times of brokenness provide us with the
opportunity to touch the hearts of others.

THE LAST THING WE think about when we are carried into a storm is how God will use it to minister to others one day. If you're like me, you could care less about helping someone else when your life is turned upside down. But that is exactly what He does through our dark valleys. He prepares in us a blessing to give others.

We give out of what God has given us. He wants to set us free so He can use our lives to set others free. When He brings life into you, He wants you to give that life to someone else as well.

Let's go back to the story of Joseph. God knew what He was doing with Joseph's life even when Joseph didn't have a clue.

Joseph endured great trials. He was thrown in a pit. He was sold into slavery. He was falsely accused. He was thrown in prison. Not the picture of a great testimony, right? But what

God did through these trials transformed our view of the trials altogether.

> "But now, don't be upset, and don't be angry with yourselves for selling me to this place. It was God who sent me here ahead of you to preserve your lives. This famine that has ravaged the land for two years will last five more years and there will be neither plowing nor harvesting. God has sent me ahead of you to keep you and your families alive and to preserve many survivors. So, you see, it was God who sent me here, not you! And He is the one who made me an adviser to Pharaoh—the manager of his entire palace and the governor of all Egypt."
> Genesis 45:5-8

There we see purpose to what Joseph endured. Because he had been where he was, he was able to keep his brothers alive. His position allowed him to care for his brothers and their families. While I'm sure at the time he didn't enjoy the sufferings he endured, he was able to see in the end how they were to be used for the better. There was purpose to the pain.

It's never easy to see purpose in the pain. When we were going through infertility, I never saw purpose. I certainly didn't see me ministering to other women because of it. At the time, I didn't care. But now, God uses this over and over again in my life to minister to others. As a matter of fact, even while I was still battling infertility, He opened up doors for me to minister to others out of what I had already learned.

That doesn't make me any better than anyone else, it just shows that He used my brokenness to minister to other women who were experiencing the same brokenness. And since then He has allowed my path to cross with many other woman the same way.

God will use the things we go through to touch others. He turns our mess into messages that bring Him glory. That's what He did for me. He turned my mess into a message of hope. He turned my test into a testimony of His faithfulness. He turned my trial into a triumph through His grace and mercy. And He did it with others in mind.

What I'm walking through now with my children, I may not understand it all, but I know that He has a bigger purpose than me. He has other mothers in mind that may need some encouragement. I want Him to accomplish His purposes in me so that when the time comes, I can give encouragement to them.

The book of Hebrews is filled with so many wonderful testimonies. Especially chapter eleven. It's filled with story after story of examples of faith by the saints of old. We see verse after verse that tell us of amazing amounts of courage and faith that these people portrayed and what God did through it. It is our chapter that is meant to build faith within us. We see their lives and their stories all through out scripture, and it is meant for us. We see their heartbreaks, we see their failures, we see their storms that they encounter, and it is meant to be a tool for us to see what can happen when we step out onto the waves of adversity and walk towards Him. It is meant to show us how even the darkest of nights can be redeemed through Him.

Their times of brokenness are used as a way to minister to us through our own.

I love how the very next chapter in Hebrews starts out:

"Therefore, since we are surrounded by such a
huge cloud of witnesses to the life of faith…"
Hebrews 12:1a

It's like our own personal group of cheerleaders cheering us on to the finish. They encourage us to keep going, to persevere and to never give up. Their lives do that for us. The example they lived. The things they went through. It's what the bible is all about - giving us examples to follow and to navigate our lives.

I mentioned before about running and marathons. The thing I loved the most in the marathon is the crowd support you get. At the start of the race it's packed with bystanders all clapping and yelling and cheering for you as you start the 26.2 mile journey. It gets your adrenaline pumping and makes you feel like you can actually do this thing.

As you proceed on further in the race, the cheers are what become most valuable to you.

I can still remember as we hit some of the later mile markers it became harder to keep going at times. It was always the coming up on some casual bystanders along the way that would give you just a little pep to keep trying. But one particular moment still stands out the most.

It was about mile eighteen, if I remember correctly. The crowds had been dwindling along the way. Occasionally, I would come upon a person who would be standing along the road offering encouragement. But at this particular place, a group of high school cross country kids had made a tunnel for the runners to go through. They lined the sides and as I ran through, they held out their hands to give high fives and lots of cheers. I ran through that and gained a new determination. It was a group of people cheering me on, giving me hope and offering encouragement. It was great.

During those last few miles it was the hardest. I mean, think about it: when you are out there all alone, quitting becomes an attractive option. You have no one telling you that you can do this. All you have is your mind and the voices going through it. And then, just when you think you may give up, you hear someone from the side of the road shouting an encouraging word for you. Or you come up to the next mile marker and the person there tells you that you're almost finished, keep going, don't quit. Or there are people offering water to help your thirst. It makes all the difference in the world when you have someone cheering you on.

Then when you reach that last mile and you hit that final turn, you see that same crowd that you saw at the start line, all lined up shouting as loud as they can, cheering you on to the finish line. They know the finish line is just around the corner and they want you to cross it. Let me just say, that when you hear all the shouts and the cheers, something happens inside of you.

You've been running for a long time. Some runners get through it in a couple of hours. In my case, I had been running non stop for over four hours at the twenty six mile point. I was exhausted. I felt like my legs were going to break into a million pieces. It took everything I had to put one foot in front of the other. However as I made that final turn and heard all the cheers and crowds of people telling me I COULD make it, I found a final burst of adrenaline that caused me to dig deeper than I ever had and push myself harder. I crossed the finish line strong. Exhausted, but strong.

That's what happens to us. In the most trying times of our battles, God sends people to cheer us on, to encourage us and to tell us that we can make it. And it's through this encouragement that we find the will to finish strong. Yes, we may be exhausted when all is said and done, but we cross the finish line standing and with our heads held high.

I don't know about you, but I want to be that kind of cheerleader for someone. I want to be there on the sidelines of their life and when they are at their weakest, I want to encourage them to keep going. I want to offer water when they are thirsty. I want my life to be an example of how you can overcome, how you can make it. So if what I'm going through hurts at the moment, I know in the end it will all be for His glory and my pain seems so very worth it.

So, we walk through darkness, we survive the storms of life and then He takes what we learned through those times and uses it to help others. Our seasons of brokenness are used to minister to others going through the same thing.

> "All praise to the God and Father of our Master,
> Jesus the Messiah! Father of all mercy! God of all
> healing counsel! He comes alongside us when we
> go through hard times, and before you know it,
> he brings us alongside someone else who is going
> through hard times so that we can be there for that
> person just as God was there for us. We have plenty
> of hard times that come from following the Messiah,
> but no more so than the good times of his healing
> comfort—we get a full measure of that, too."
> 2 Corinthians 1:3-5

Remember what you learn on your journey. Hide it in your heart so that when the time comes and God brings someone your way who is battling the same things you have, you will be ready to share your story and what God did for you to help them find their way. Never underestimate what your testimony can do for someone else.

I'm so grateful for what I went through. It has provided many open doors for me to share Jesus with others. It has provided an avenue for me to share hope and offer encouragement. It wasn't an easy road to travel at the time, but it has been worth it seeing what God has done with it in His hands.

He will do the same for you if you choose to follow Him along the path. Let Him be your guide through the journey, and He will lead you to others who are trying to find hope along the way. You'll be there to offer what God has so graciously given you. He fills our cups so we can pour it out into others.

You've ran your race, now it's time to cheer others along the way in theirs.

Chapter 12

SUNRISE

"Weeping may last for the night, but .
joy comes in the morning."

Psalms 30:5

THERE'S SOMETHING ABOUT SEEING a sunrise that never ceases to amaze me and take my breath away. It is so majestic and powerful and the colors that come just before it rises are beyond beautiful. They paint a picture to get you ready, and then before you know it, here comes the sun, bringing with it all its glory. It's amazing.

So with the way the time is now, I haven't gotten to see many sunrises on my runs lately. It's always one of the things I love most. Especially on long run days. Today was one of them. I had thirteen miles to do. We usually do some of the longer runs starting at the TVA Trail and go up to the Marriott and across the dam and back. Well today as we were crossing over the dam, you could see the moments just before the sun was about to rise. The sky was beautiful. It had pink and yellow and orange tones that almost gave me chills. You could see the light coming from beneath it, setting the stage for a gorgeous sunrise.

As I was running, I started thinking about sunrises and why I love them so much. Then I realized that it's because of what the sunrise stands for. The sun rises after a period of darkness and night. It brings light to darkness.

Just like the sun rises after a time of darkness, it reflects what happens in our lives as well. We all go through periods of darkness. Times when we can't see in front of us because it's so dark. Situations bring despair and hopelessness. It feels cold and empty. But just at the right time, the Son begins to rise in our lives. We see the glimpses of color just before and this brings us hope. Then, in all of His majesty and glory, He begins to rise within our dark moments. The darkness we were surrounded with begins to fade in the presence of His glorious light. Before we know it, the darkness is gone and we are surrounded by His light within us. WOW!!!

I don't know about you, but that just gives me hope. Hope to keep enduring every hour of the night I am in. Why? Because hope is on the horizon. HE is on the horizon. And that hope pulls me through every moment I stand in darkness because I know it is temporary. I am so thankful for His light that rises in my darkest moments and surrounds me with His presence. I can't imagine going through the fire and NOT knowing that my help comes from God.

Everything I've learned about walking through darkness all revolves and centers around one word when it all comes down to it. And that word? It's faith. We saw how Abraham taught us all about what it means to have faith. And not just any faith. He showed us a faith that obeys. He showed us a faith that overrides doubt. He showed us a faith that birthed expectancy.

For Abraham, faith meant saying yes to God and following Him into the wilderness. He followed even though he had no idea where he was going. He just followed based on the fact that he knew if God was leading, He would take him to where he needed to be.

Sarah and Abraham show us what it means to walk in faith and to obey whole heartedly. Just think, if they had chosen not to obey, if they had chosen to stay in their comfort zone in the land of Ur, think of what they would have missed out on. They would have forfeited the inheritance of the promise to stay in a land of comfort and familiarity. It makes me wonder, what have I missed out on the times I have failed to obey? It makes me wonder, what would I have forfeited if I had not chosen to stay on the path and allow God to lead me through the darkness? I know three blessings I might have missed out on altogether if I had chosen a different path. Boy am I glad I kept following.

Our journey of faith develops something within us. It develops courage. It's a courage that comes from following Him to places we do not know, into areas we do not understand, and a land that we do not comprehend. But here's what should give us hope amidst it—He will never lead us where He has not gone before us. When He goes before us, He prepares the way. Yes, we may walk into uncharted places. We may travel down roads we have not seen, covered by a cloud of darkness. But we do not walk alone. He will never lead us into a storm or down a path that He will not go there with us. Even in the midst of a storm, we are not alone. Though He may lead us into that storm, He doesn't send us out in a boat and expect us to fend for ourselves. If He knows the storm is coming, you can be confident that in the middle of that storm, you will see Him walking towards you.

And one more thing, He won't send you into a storm without having a divine revelation awaiting you when it's over. Just like the disciples saw Jesus and the truth of Who He was when the storm ended, so will you. He will reveal Himself to you through the storms and when all is said and done, you'll be able to kneel before Him and declare that surely, He IS the Son of God.

Whatever your situation looks like, you can be sure that He has a divine agenda at work. I can't tell you what His plan is, or what He will speak to you in the midst of it. To be completely honest, even when you submit to what He's doing, I can't tell you that things will turn out the way you hoped they would. What I can tell you, though, is to let Him be God. Trust His sovereignty, trust His heart. He never has a plan to harm you. His plans are always to prosper you and bring you hope.

Even though we may not see the next step in front of us, remember that He has gone before you to make the crooked places straight. He will lead and guide you. He will direct you.

> "I'll take the hand of those who don't know the way,
> who can't see where they're going. I'll be a personal
> guide to them, directing them through unknown
> country. I'll be right there to show them what roads
> to take, make sure they don't fall into the ditch.
> These are the things I'll be doing for them—sticking
> with them, not leaving them for a minute."
> Isaiah 42:16 The Message

He will lead you by the way of peace. We need not worry about what our future holds. We only need to trust that He will direct our steps, that He will be beside us all the way. Even in the middle of the storm, He will be there.

Sunrises are like new beginnings. They are new chapters that are yet to unfold. It reminds me of my house. We built the house we had been living in. When we decided to move back to Alabama, my father gave us some land and we built our first house. It was a story in and of itself! But it was a special place for us because we did so much of the work in the house ourselves. It was ours. We made some beautiful memories there.

But as the boys grew and became involved, the location of our house was not the best. It wasn't that we lived extremely far out, but where we did live was the opposite direction of everything we did. So after months of praying about it, we felt God led us to put the house up for sale and move into the city.

It was back at the end of September last year when it finally sold. It had been on the market for about two months and finally a couple came and looked at it and fell in love. They offered a contract, we accepted, and in a little over a month we were packing and moving out.

I still remember the last week in the house. It was a little sad. We had lived here for over six years. We built memories. We had stake in this house. But at last, we were ending this chapter of our lives and starting a new one. The seasons were changing for our family and our lives.

Just like in all the seasons changing, there are always things that take place upon every new season. There are always changes coming. Leaves change. Colors change. Temperatures change. Weather changes. It's all full of changes. Some changes represent life. Some changes represent death. Flowers bloom in the spring. They die in the winter. Leaves grow and are green and healthy in the spring and summer. They die and fall to the ground in the fall and winter. Everything changes with each passing season. But all of the changes serve a greater purpose. With each death, there is always life that springs forth in a new season.

And so it is with our lives. Seasons will change. Things will come and go Flowers will bloom and flowers will die. Ecclesiastes tells us it is certain.

"For everything there is a season, a time
for every activity under heaven.
A time to be born and a time to die.
A time to plant and a time to harvest.
A time to kill and a time to heal.
A time to tear down and a time to build up.
A time to cry and a time to laugh.
A time to grieve and a time to dance.
A time to scatter stones and a time to gather stones.
A time to embrace and a time to turn away.
A time to search and a time to quit searching.
A time to keep and a time to throw away.
A time to tear and a time to mend.
A time to be quiet and a time to speak.
A time to love and a time to hate.
A time for war and a time for peace."
Ecclesiastes 3:1-8 NLT

There will be seasons in every part of our life. Some will be full of life; some will be about things dying. But no matter the season, we know it is only for a time. Before we know it, the season will change and something new will take place. It is part of God's divine plan.

I have walked through some difficult days. But looking back, I wouldn't want anything different for my life. I wouldn't trade the years I battled infertility for anything in this world. I came to know Jesus in a way I may not have otherwise. I wouldn't trade the waiting period for anything. I came to understand that I'm not alone in my waiting and that He has much to show me during the waiting periods in my life. I wouldn't trade having children who have their own battles to face now with behavioral and emotional issues. While this particular journey is really just starting, I know that I do not walk alone. If He placed these children in my care, and He chose these three boys to complete our family, He knew what He was doing. He's not surprised by anything happening in our lives right now. If He's not surprised by it, then I won't be worried about it. If I really believe that my times are in His hands, then I have to trust that He will carry me through to the end. Though I may never see my children live without these issues, I still choose to trust Him. I still choose to follow and offer Him my everything.

I've seen Him in the good times of my life. I've given Him my praise when my life is full of abundance and blessings. I've offered all I have when my life is full of smiles and laughter.

Because I've come to know Him in the hard times, too, then when dark days come my way, when storm clouds roll in, when my road takes a detour to an unknown path, I will still lift my hands and declare that He alone is the only One worthy to receive my praise. I'll praise Him when my circumstances tell me I should not.

At times the dark valleys of my life have seemed overwhelming and almost caused me to lose hope and give up. But then I remember the sunrise, and I know that weeping may last for a night, but joy will come in the morning. I know that He is about to rise in all of His glory and shine His light into the dark times of my life. And that sets my heart at peace and fills me with strength to endure every moment until I see His deliverance.

> "I'll go ahead of you, clearing and paving the road. I'll break down bronze city gates, smash padlocks, kick down barred entrances. I'll lead you to buried treasures, secret caches of valuables—Confirmations that it is, in fact, I, God, the God of Israel, who calls you by your name. It's because of my dear servant Jacob, Israel my chosen, That I've singled you out, called you by name, and given you this privileged work."
> Isaiah 45:2 The Message

I may not know what my future holds. I may not understand why I am on the paths I am traveling. I may be surrounded by darkness on all sides. But I still have hope.

You may find yourself in the same place. You may find yourself right in the middle of the most intense storm of your life. You may have been given a divine detour off the path you were traveling. But I hope that through the journey we've been on together, you have learned to not just LIVE through your dark times, but to LEARN from them. That you find your pearl of great price through your pain. My prayer for you is that you are able to put your questions aside, that you can lay down your agendas, and buckle up on the caravan He has you on at the moment. Let Him carry you down the path that leads to where His abundance is awaiting you. When you can't see things other than your own perspective, let Daddy pick you up and put you on His shoulders so you can see things from His perspective. Take all of your most valuable dreams and things you hold dear and bury them at His feet. In the middle of your darkness, you find yourself with an audience of One, even if you can't see Him at the time.

And what do you do when you find yourself standing on top of the graves of all you've buried at His feet? What do you do when you have nothing but your heart left to offer up to the One worthy of your alabaster box? What do you do when you find yourself alone, in the midst of darkness? What then? Then you dance.

REFERENCES

Chapter 6

Kairos - In God's Appointed Time, by Kathy L. McFarland.
January 13, 2008
http://iknowjesuslovesme.blogspot.com/2008/01/kairos-
in-gods-appointed-time.html

Wikipedia, "Kairos."
http://en.wikipedia.org/wiki/kairos

To continue with Stacy in her journey, follow her blog at:

www.stacyfulton.blogspot.com

To contact Stacy, email her at:

dailyendurance@yahoo.com

90010